ID0983344

The Diplomatic Persuaders

The Diplomatic Persuaders

New Role of the Mass Media
in International Relations

JOHN LEE, EDITOR
Associate Professor of Journalism
University of Arizona, Tucson

CONSULTANT
Washington Journalism Center
Washington, D. C.

John Wiley & Sons, Inc.
New York • London • Sydney • Toronto

Library of Congress Catalog Card Number: 68-30916
SBN 471 52210 4
Printed in the United States of America

To Ray E. Hiebert, who warned me that editing a book can be tougher than writing one and who was (as he nearly always has been) absolutely right.

Series Preface

In a democratic society there is no more important principle than the people's right to know about their government and its obligation to keep the people informed. The role of the press and communication in the governing process has been important since the earliest days of the nation.

In the modern mass society of an international power communication between government and people through a complex and often instantaneous means of transmission has vital implications and consequences. The explosive impact of the mass media on the political and governmental process has brought about changes in politics, public administration, and international relations.

The interrelationship between government and communication has many new dimensions that must be explored and understood. The "Wiley Series on Government and Communication" was conceived to probe and provide greater understanding of those new dimensions.

Some of the books in the series deal with the way in which governments (local, national, and international) communicate with the people, either directly or through the press and mass media.

Other books in the series discuss the way in which the people, usually through the press and mass media, obtain information from government.

Finally, some of the series books treat of problems that arise at that intersection of society at which government and people meet through the media. These are problems of the social, economic, legal, and political implications of the communication process when dealing with government, the problems of restriction and censorship, of distortion and propaganda, of freedom and national security, and of organization and technology.

Certainly the future of democracy may depend to a large extent on the success with which we understand and meet the problems created by the relationship between government and communication in a new age.

RAY ELDON HIEBERT
Series Editor

Preface

In the tranquil days before World War I foreign policy was decided by a handful of specialists in striped pants closeted in quiet rooms. Diplomats spoke discreetly with one another over matters of mutual concern, made concessions, and drew up documents of sweeping importance. Governments rose and fell on the scratch of a pen without the public's knowing or perhaps really caring about such events. Diplomacy was a very private affair.

In the last half century, however, a great social and political convulsion has taken place. With the proliferation of communication, information has expanded and become diffused. The man in the street, the *calle,* the *rue,* the *strada,* and the *strasse* has begun to pay attention to what is going on around him and to form opinions. Governments—particularly democracies—are frequently forced to abide by these opinions.

If the force of public opinion, however, is to influence public policy in issues that may involve national security and the safety of millions of people, it must naturally be an informed public opinion. It is no longer possible for high-level statesmen to glide through the lofty avenues of diplomacy, trailed by first, second, and third secretaries in perfect protocol alignment. A government, to survive, must supplement formal government-to-government relations with an approach to the people. The people must be given access to the facts and to the alternatives. They must be made aware of the intricacies of domestic and foreign policy.

To meet this challenge governments around the world have turned to a totally new concept of international diplomacy. This is the age of public diplomacy, the era of people-to-people dialogues, the day of human communications.

Nor is it sufficient only to inform ourselves and our friends. International opinion wields incredible power, and we must inform the people of other nations as well, allies and enemies alike. The government that fails to do so may find itself inarticulate in the face of world opinion.

In the white-hot glare of present-day publicity and press attention an ambassador in his public appearances no longer makes brief standard speeches that pledge "friendship between our two countries." He is more likely to deal in solid factual language designed to orient or sway public opinion in the host country. Even diplomatic notes are often couched in terms designed more to influence the public mind than to influence the recipient government.

Mention of an ambassadorial speech in a newspaper or invitations to a tea at the chancellory are still methods by which people in a host country may be reached, but they are only very small eddies in the information flow that now emanates from embassies. Embassies are approaching the public mind through the press, embassy publications, libraries, movies, lectures, trade fairs, eye-to-eye contact, and even a few casual martini lunches with pertinent newsmen. This type of open diplomacy calls for the guidance of a professional—a career press or information counselor.

Every national capital in the world with embassies and legations has its corps of information counselors whose job it is to reach the public, largely through the open door provided by the burgeoning media. Perhaps nowhere in the world is the press or the public more accessible than in the United States. Washington, D.C., has become not only the nation's news center but the mecca of world news as well. Representatives of every major news service and news syndicate, correspondents from each of the great newspapers around the world, reporters from many of the smaller newspapers, radio and television newsmen, and stringers for chains of small and middle-sized publications all flock to Washington to touch its pulse.

This, the widest of all open doors to the public mind, is not overlooked by the governments of the world. Among the 116 nations represented by embassies and legations in Washington each has at least one of its diplomatic personnel designated to handle contact with the media, even if only on a part-time basis. The number varies with the size of the embassy; some of the larger embassies have staffs that would rival those of good-sized newspaper city rooms.

Even though the concept of public diplomacy is accepted by a majority of governments and its fruits are generally utilized by newsmen, few attempts have been made to describe how it functions or to indicate its impact. It is important to move toward a fully fleshed understanding of what we are being told, how it is being told, and what effect the telling may have on world politics.

In the spring of 1967 the Washington Journalism Center and the American University in Washington, D.C., offered a cooperative series of 20 seminars. Press attachés and information counselors from 17 of Washington's embassies spoke. In addition, an expert on Red China evaluated the propaganda and persuasion techniques of a country not accredited in Washington; the deputy director of the United States Information Agency defined this nation's role in other capitals of the world; and an information specialist of the United Nations described the immense informational setup of an intergovernmental organization.

At the end of the seminars 16 of the talks were drawn up in chapter form by the participants for inclusion in this book. There were casualties; for instance, Mohamed Habib of the United Arab Republic was forced by circumstances to drop out of the lineup when two days before a chapter-taping session his government broke relations with the United States as a result of the 1967 Middle East conflict. Israel's Dan Pattir had a similarly unexpected call on his time because of the same crisis. Events at home also caused the withdrawal of John Nicolopoulos of the Greek Embassy after the military coup in Athens. Life for press attachés can be hectic.

In their quieter moments press and information attachés are generally engaged in a threefold job designed (a) to further the foreign policies of their governments, (b) to combat hostile propaganda, and (c) to inform their own governments of foreign attitudes. In pursuit of the first two of these goals the attachés use such practical techniques as the press release and the press conference. Like nondiplomatic public relations practitioners, many of the press and information attachés—dubbed "copy-pushers in striped pants" by one of their number, Cvijeto Job of the Yugoslav Embassy—spent their early careers on news-papers. This helps them to deal effectively with the press. Among the 20 seminar speakers, for example, 15 were former newsmen.

The discharge of a diplomatic press counselor's duties can be classified as sophisticated public relations; on occasion it is called pure propaganda—but one man's "information" is another man's "propaganda," depending on one's point of view. In this country many people frown automatically at the word "propaganda" be-cause of its recent (since World War II and Joseph Goebbels' Ministry of Propaganda) connotation; it is now what is often called a loaded word. Yet many information specialists, includ-ing some of the writers of these chapters, use the words "infor-mation" and "propaganda" interchangeably.

Use of the press to help influence the public mind is perhaps the most formidable of weapons in the public diplomat's arsenal because of the large numbers that may be reached; but just as important as the media is the theory of person-to-person commu-nication. This technique, for example, is used by the United States Information Agency on a worldwide basis. According to Deputy Director Robert Akers, information specialists from the United States may go directly to individuals and talk to them (a labor leader, a college professor whose lectures indicate he may be hostile to the United States, a student, a student group, a gov-ernment leader). Sometimes differences may be resolved by care-ful explanations and thoughtful answers to questions. There is a definite human limitation to how many people can be reached in this manner but the results can be most important.

In contrast to the extensive machinery used by such large in-formation programs as the USIA are the low-budget approaches of smaller countries described by Po Sung Kim in the chapter on Korea. Korea is forced to rely most strongly on what Mr. Kim calls "jujitsu public relations"—using the weight of the other fellow to advantage, the "other fellow" in Korea's case being the commercial firms, groups, and individuals in the United States interested in the welfare of Korea.

Not all press counselors, however, can expect friendly reactions from the people or press of a host country. All too often the press counselors must work with an indifferent or even hostile press, and, as is inherent in the situation, their attempts at communication, no matter how overt or purely motivated, can sometimes be misunderstood. Pakistan's S.N. Qutb, for example, once gained brief public notice as a spy. Serving as a press attaché in India before coming to Washington, he had gone to visit the editor of an Indian magazine that ran considerable adverse material on Pakistan, had chatted with him, and, leaving, had invited him to dinner. The editor declined. In the very next edition of the magazine a story described how the editor had managed to forestall the attempt of a spy "to lure him into some dark place," Mr. Qutb says. On the cover, in big boxed type, was the blurb "Pakistan's Master Spy."

Because press attachés are a tenacious lot, Mr. Qutb did not allow the matter to rest there. The two men met many times after their first encounter and became friends. The editor never stopped criticizing, but his attacks lessened in vehemence. According to Mr. Qutb, this is the only way to handle a hostile press— to continue to meet the editors and to try to persuade them to see both sides of a question.

A hostile press can be expected as a natural element any time two countries are involved in some sort of confrontation. The presses of India and Pakistan, Israel and the Arabic countries, Rhodesia and the black African countries all present hostile faces to one another. Nor is a hostile press restricted to countries outside the United States. As will be seen, press attachés from communist embassies feel that their press pronouncements are automatically met in this country with suspicion and hostility. One communist bloc press attaché commented, "You can talk about the iron curtain or the silk curtain or the bamboo curtain all you want. It can be just as difficult breaking through the *democratic* curtain."

More often than hostility, however, the press in the United

States is accused of indifference. In the chapters that follow at least two old friends of this country express feelings that they are taken for granted or ignored altogether by the American press. Others indicate that the American press is sometimes too indifferent to check the facts, thus burdening the press attaché with images that will not go away. The problem of a faulty image is a standard headache of the press attaché. Many feel that their image problems result from a failure of their own information machinery to convey their message. Others feel the problem rests at the doorstep of the American press and its concept of crisis reporting. "Denmark," a foreign correspondent remarked during the course of the seminars, "has made page one of the American newspapers only twice in the last quarter-century—once when Germany invaded her, and once when the little mermaid lost her head."

Beyond the first two goals of the press attaché—furthering the foreign policies and images of his government and combating hostile propaganda—is the third goal of informing his own government of foreign attitudes. This is basically an information-retrieval job. The press attaché, with an already busy schedule, must read constantly, must scan as many major publications as possible, and search for items about his country that will give an indication of public or governmental attitudes toward his homeland. As a bonus, the press attaché, like any good public relations man, learns from his reading which publications are using the press material he is providing, which publications might need straightening out on facts, and which might be interested in additional material on his country. Japan takes the further step of using public opinion polls to determine public interest. The Japanese press and information people have discovered through the polls that a large percentage of the people in America's Midwest take very little interest in Japan. The Japanese information people feel, therefore, that it is not economically sound to spend a great deal of time and money in the dissemination of materials to people in this broad area. Consequently, they concentrate their information flow on the East and West Coast areas, where they feel the interest is higher.

Regardless of the tools they choose for implementation, the underlying goal of the information programs now being undertaken by the governments of the world is to persuade. The nations are saying, "Be interested in me. Learn to understand me, my history, my motivations, and my contributions, and through this understanding become persuaded that my ambitions are not incongruous with your own interests." We may not always agree on the congruity of national ambitions, but we must agree that the attempt to persuade is an indispensable force in the world today. These diplomatic public relations practitioners are not selling a cigarette, a soft drink, or a mouthwash. They are selling national images, understanding, and, in some cases, possible world survival.

As the late Edward R. Murrow, when director of the USIA, said: "If this country believes that the end of the day will be carried not by force of arms but by force of persuasion, the job we do is a key to our survival. I for one am persuaded that we have no alternative; we must persuade or perish in the attempt."

JOHN LEE

Tucson, Arizona
June 1968

Contents

1

An Indispensable Diplomacy

ROBERT W. AKERS
DEPUTY DIRECTOR
U. S. INFORMATION AGENCY

ROBERT WOOD AKERS was born in Topeka, Kansas, in 1905, but he considers Texas his home. He was educated at the University of Texas (after first attending Washburn College in Topeka and the University of Chicago). He has been associated with many Texas newspapers, including the *San Antonio Evening News* and the *Beaumont Enterprise*, where he has held positions as reporter, city editor, managing editor, and editor-in-chief.

His newspaper career was not without interruptions. During World War II he saw combat service in northern France as a captain in the 70th Infantry Division. In 1953 he was sent by the U.S. government on a four-month lecture tour in India, the Philippines, Korea, and Japan. In August 1965 he was appointed Deputy Director of the United States Information Agency.

BEFORE the end of World War II there had never been, in time of peace, any element of the United States Government responsible for communicating with the peoples of other countries. When the United States Information Agency was established as an independent agency in August 1953, many questioned whether it was necessary or whether it was, indeed, in keeping with American traditions.

Yet not too long ago Secretary of State Dean Rusk stated, "Today, we in the State Department consider the information program as an indispensable dimension of American diplomacy. Our information activities demonstrate our respect for the opinions of people as well as their governments."

This is surely a dramatic and revealing twentieth century development—and one that is not uniquely American, but nearly universal.

If you study the current Washington Diplomatic List, you will find that 65 of the 116 countries represented include on their embassy staffs officers concerned with disseminating information to the American people. Nor does this tell the whole story; many countries list only the diplomatic titles of staff members, such as "second secretary," without specifying their functions.

On this same current Diplomatic List, you can find one Middle Eastern country whose Washington embassy staff includes a cultural counselor, six cultural attachés, a press counselor, a press attaché, a public relations counselor, and a public relations attaché.

If studying the Diplomatic List does not appeal to you, try tuning in a shortwave radio some night. You will find the air literally crackling with voices that represent various nations, talking to people of other nations in the languages of those nations. Nearly 3500 shortwave transmitters are used in this nocturnal competition for the ears—and minds—of people everywhere.

Understand that I do not write critically of those activities. I deplore attempts of any government to erect barriers to the free access of its citizens to information, and I applaud the efforts of any government to get its story across to the peoples of other countries. President Lyndon Johnson has observed, "Today the advancing technology of communications presents all of the human race the first real opportunity to encompass the world with the understanding that will finally assure peace for all mankind."

So that you may more fully appreciate what I have to say to you about the U.S. Information Agency, I suggest the following.

O We first briefly review what has happened in the area of international relations to make it possible for the work of an agency that did not exist 15 years ago to be described by the Secretary of State as "a major dimension of diplomacy."

O We then try to look ahead to see what "the advancing technology of communications," of which President Johnson has spoken, holds in store for us, with a view to determining our true ability to take advantage of the opportunity it represents for world peace.

Of the several twentieth century developments that have transformed the conduct of international relations, one demands to be cited first. It affected not only the conduct but the very nature of international relations. It began in the early 1920's, shortly after the end of World War I.

Traditionally, and the tradition went back several centuries, diplomacy followed certain fixed rules, one of which was that governments talked only to governments. Then, in the early 1920's, through the medium of shortwave radio, governments began to address themselves to the *peoples* of other countries, *in the languages* of those countries, *without consulting the other governments concerned*. Now, four decades later, this has ceased to be a radical departure from tradition and is no longer limited to the medium of radio. It has become a commonplace fact of international life, and in the realm of diplomacy nothing will ever again be the same.

Another twentieth century development, a revolution in communications, has made this development possible. Although throughout history there have been occasions on which a government communicated with the citizens of another country, as Benjamin Franklin did in France for the United States during our Revolutionary War, it was always on a limited scale. The same thing is now feasible on a massive scale.

Radio probably affords the most striking illustration of this development. Radio recognizes neither distance nor borders nor official decrees. It demands no special training or education on the part of the listener, not even literacy (UNESCO studies indicate that two out of every three adults in the world today are illiterate). With the advent of the transistor, there are few people anywhere without access to a radio—now small, portable, battery-powered, and cheap.

The system produced by this communications revolution, the system of mass media, has done much more than make it possible for governments to talk to people (their own and others); it has done something else, with an equally striking effect on international relations. Through the mass media—especially radio, but also motion pictures and television—millions upon millions of people have acquired an awareness of the world over the next hill or beyond the horizon. They have learned of better ways of life, have realized that something other than fate has kept them in bondage, have come to realize that government's power is no more than a reflection of their own. They have come to aspire, and governments have learned that legitimate aspirations of the people cannot be ignored. Charles W. Cole, former President of Amherst College, who was for three years American Ambassador to Chile, has referred to "political awareness and economic expectations . . . multiplied tenfold by the advent of the transistor radio." "Today," continues Mr. Cole, "the undernourished Indians of a Bolivian village, a hundred miles from a power line, can listen to the exhortations of a *politico* in La Paz."

The mass media, in other words, have, on the one hand, replaced apathy with opinion and acquiescence with aspiration. On the other hand, the mass media represent the instruments by which responsible leaders can guide those opinions and aspirations, or by which enemies—internal and external—can subvert them.

Although space does not permit a complete cataloguing of all the great changes that have transformed the nature and conduct of diplomacy, there is a third, which would have to be included in any list, no matter how brief. It is a phenomenon of people, cities, and countries.

If the present rate of growth of world population had existed since the time of Christ, there would now be one person for every square foot of land on this planet. Between now and 1980 the world will have to feed *1 billion more persons*, and *four out of five* of these will be born in countries even now incapable of feeding their present populations. President Johnson has summed it up by declaring that "man's greatest problem is the fearful race between food and population."

There has been a movement of people to cities. There are 80 cities in the world with a population of a million or more; 20 years ago there were only 30. A quarter of the world's population now lives in cities of 20,000 or more; this represents a 35 percent increase in 10 years. On the one hand, this means an ever-increasing mass-media audience, because access to the media is always easier and more extensive in urban centers. On the other, it obviously means more non-food-producing consumers of food.

Nations, too, have been multiplying. We need only consider the United Nations, whose membership has more than doubled in the brief two decades since its birth. More nations in a world that is physically the same size it has always been inevitably mean more points of friction and more chance of conflict. Under such circumstances, continuous communication among the peoples of the world becomes not merely highly desirable, but absolutely essential.

Now, let us turn toward the future.

To understand what lies ahead, we must view it within the framework of what has gone before. In the area of international communication not only the tremendous advances are significant, but perhaps even more the increasing rapidity with which those advances have been made. Similarly, the wonders of what lies ahead are equaled, if not surpassed, by the speed with which we are approaching the day of those miracles.

Today we can pick up a telephone and talk to someone 10,000 miles away. We can speak into a microphone at USIA's broadcast service, the Voice of America, and be heard by someone in a jungle halfway around the world—someone who, perhaps, has never traveled 30 miles from where he was born.

When an American space capsule splashes down, more than 100 million people thousands of miles from the scene see it on their television screens, *as it happens.*

We tend to take all this for granted, yet when Morse invented the telegraph in 1840 (not so long ago against the background of recorded history), it marked the first time a message of any complexity could travel great distances faster than a messenger; and the tiny transistor of which we have spoken, which has so revolutionized the process of governing, did not exist 15 years ago.

Now, looking ahead, let us limit ourselves to just three of the scores of breakthroughs in communication: satellites, integrated circuits, and lasers, representing totally different technologies yet closely related through their contributions to communication.

Just a decade ago the first artificial satellite had yet to be launched successfully. Today there are more than a dozen communications satellites orbiting the earth. As for their significance, consider just a single aspect: two new "commercial" communications satellites were orbited in 1967 at a cost of about 14 million dollars, each satellite having a capacity of over 300 circuits. (COMSAT's Lani Bird II and Atlantic II—"Canary Bird.") By comparison, the biggest transatlantic cable, installed in 1966, cost 145 million dollars and has a capacity of only 138 circuits.

Young as it is, revolutionary as its accomplishments have been, the transistor is on the verge of being replaced. Tiny chips of silicon on which circuits have been baked are known as integrated circuits, or "IC's" or just plain "chips." One of these IC's is no larger than one of the tiny holes in a window screen and is thin enough to thread through a needle. It requires only a fraction of a volt for power, and it is hundreds of times more reliable than even the dependable transistor. Just a thimbleful of these chips can provide enough circuitry for dozens of computers or thousands of radios.

Serious work on beams of coherent light, known as lasers, began a mere five years ago. Capable of instantaneously drilling a hole through steel or of repairing a detached retina in an eye, the laser's countless uses range from industry to surgery. Its communication potential can be summed up in the fact that a single laser beam can carry more information than all the radio circuits in the United States, combined.

The following are some of the developments we can anticipate from the three just described.

O Available circuitry will increase beyond our present powers of imagination. One primitive satellite—Early Bird—doubled (to about 400) the available circuits between Europe and the United States. Engineers foresee, in the near future, satellites with 10,000 circuits each.

O Lasers alone will have a capacity millions of times greater than today's most advanced systems, and the laser can carry electronic signals of different media, simultaneously.

O As the versatility of communications satellites increases, it will become possible to broadcast directly to individual television sets and radio receivers in homes or in classrooms anywhere on earth.

O The miniaturization made possible by the chips—the integrated circuits—will make standard equipment of wrist radios, each unit capable of being dialed from any other unit. As somebody has said, "We'll soon be at the point where, if your party doesn't answer, he's dead."

O The ultimate, as seen by General David Sarnoff, will be a master grid that can be linked to any system of electronic communication, by means of which every person on earth will have access, at any time, to any information he may require.

Within the framework of what has been discussed to this point, let me now tell you about the U.S. Information Agency, USIA.

An independent agency of the United States Government whose director is appointed by the President with the advice and consent of the Senate, the USIA is staffed by about 12,000 people; 7000 of these are foreign nationals employed by us in their own countries. The operating budget of the agency for the current fiscal year is approximately 170 million dollars. Although we find this amount adequate for our needs, I should like to mention —so that you may see this in perspective—that the amount is about 30 million dollars less than a well-known corporation spends yearly to advertise one of its products: soap.

The mission of the USIA may be stated very simply: the USIA communicates with peoples of other nations for the purpose of making American policies and actions understandable to them. To accomplish this, we realize that it is not enough simply to explain these policies and actions; we also inform other peoples of the history, traditions, culture, and way of life from which the policies and actions flow.

To accomplish its mission, the USIA thus transfers information, which is another way of saying it communicates. In so doing we hope to create and nurture understanding of ourselves abroad.

Please note that I have used the word *information, not ideology,* and I have used the word *understanding, not agreement.* Certainly we hope others will agree with us, but we also know that there are times when this is simply not possible. When Greece and Turkey struggled over Cyprus, USIS libraries were attacked —in Athens, *and* in Ankara, *and* in Nicosia. Could we reasonably expect both the Arabs and the Israelis to agree with American policy at a given time? Or the Indians and the Pakistani?

Lack of agreement is, at best, unpleasant; but lack of agreement in the absence of understanding is dangerous.

The USIA employs all channels of communication to carry out its mission. Among these channels are the mass media.

O The USIA's radio service, the Voice of America, broadcasts 810 hours a week to all parts of the world in 38 languages. Taped VOA programs, additionally, along with others produced by some of our overseas posts, are carried on local stations in other countries.

O We use magazines. In addition to the Russian- and Polish-language editions of *America Illustrated,* which are sold in the U.S.S.R. and Poland, the USIA produces *Al Hayat* for Arabic-speaking countries and French and English editions of *Topic* for the young, educated, future leaders of Africa. We also have three regional service centers—at Beirut, Manila, and Mexico City—that respond to regional needs for printed matter in local languages. In addition to pamphlets, leaflets, and posters these three centers publish 19 magazines in 14 languages for use in 111 countries.

O The USIA's motion picture and television service produces more than 1000 motion picture documentaries and television programs annually. Each year more than 700 million people see the films. The television programs have been telecast by more than 2000 TV stations in 92 countries.

○ Our 227 libraries and reading rooms in 87 countries attract 25 million visitors yearly, with students comprising the largest segment.

○ Our exhibits have achieved success in areas where we do not enjoy much freedom of action. Most recently, the exhibit *Hand Tools—USA* attracted 2½ million Hungarians, Poles, Russians, Bulgarians, and Yugoslavs at Budapest, Poznan, Kharkov, Plovdiv, and Zagreb.

I realize that statistics can be misleading, when not boring— and there are those who say it is difficult to decide which is worse. I have cited these few to provide a reference as contrast for what I say next.

You will recall that I wrote the USIA employs *all channels* of communication to achieve its objectives and that *among* these are the mass media. The fact of the matter is that, for all their miraculous efficiency, the modern mass media by themselves cannot do the job that has to be done. This has been demonstrated time and time again by social research in both the newly emerging nations (not so surprising) and the most advanced nations of the world, including our own (a great surprise to many).

The mass media must be used in planned conjunction with the most fundamental—but also the most effective—communication channel of all: the face-to-face or, if you prefer, person-to-person encounter.

This is the main reason why the USIA maintains 220 U.S. Information Service posts in 105 countries, staffed by some 1750 Americans and 7000 locally employed nationals. It is the main reason why our training program lays such heavy stress on acquisition of foreign-language capabilities. And it is the main reason why, wherever our resources permit, we do not rely solely on a post in the capital city of a country, but maintain branch posts in secondary cities and rural areas.

This, then, is the role of the USIA in the world of today. What of tomorrow?

As communications techniques improve and as new ones come into being, our communication capabilities will, of course, multiply. After the invention of the telegraph, however, when it was excitedly explained that Maine and Texas would now be able to talk to each other, Thoreau observed: "What if Maine and Texas have nothing to say to each other?" As a global communications grid takes shape, what are the nations and the peoples of the world going to say to one another? More specifically, what is the USIA, on behalf of the United States, going to say to the other people of the world?

To some extent we will continue to talk about some of the same things we now do: peace under rule of law; the true nature of our system of government, our culture, our way of life; what free enterprise really means and what kind of life it can make possible for people everywhere.

To a much greater degree, however, I am sure we shall be talking about other things, for it will be a different world in which we shall be living. With the miracles—in communications and other fields—there will be problems. Along with the challenges will come threats.

We shall thus be talking about problems of population growth; ways and means of increasing food production; poverty: the per capita income of developed countries is 2000 dollars a year. In the developing nations it is less than a tenth of that. As time passes, if nothing is done to decrease this gap, the revolution of rising expectations will be superseded by a potentially devastating revolution of rising frustrations.

I do not mean to imply that we shall simply use all the new techniques of communication endlessly to discuss these and other problems and threats. Our task will be that of *informing* people not only of the threats and problems, but also of how the threats may be met and the problems solved.

Mankind, as we have stated, is engaged in a race between population growth and food production. But man also faces, in this age of nuclear missiles, a race between communication and catastrophe.

It has only been comparatively recently that information programs have become a major dimension of diplomacy, but it will be a long, long time before they lose this stature. Communication has always been necessary to the survival of any group as a group. It has now become critical to the survival of all mankind as a species.

2

Sweden—Land of Sin, Suicide, and Socialism

SVEN FRYCHIUS
PRESS COUNSELOR
ROYAL SWEDISH EMBASSY

SVEN FRYCHIUS was born in Sweden in 1907. After studies in philosophy at the Universities of Uppsala and Lund he became a reporter, working first with daily newspapers in different parts of the country. From 1935 to 1940 he wrote for the liberal Stockholm daily *Svenska Morgonbladet*.

During World War II Mr. Frychius served in the press department of his government's information board, the last two years as department chief. This marked the beginning of a long association with the government. He has been with the Swedish Foreign Ministry since 1945. For the first 10 years, he was in the Ministry's press department. In 1955, he was named Press Attaché to the Swedish Embassy in Oslo, Norway. He served in Oslo until 1962, when he was named Press Counselor to the Swedish Embassy in Washington.

W ITH great pleasure I take the opportunity of presenting my activity in the information field in the United States. Right at the beginning I am anxious to point out that the ideological groundwork I will try to introduce is my personal philosophy, developed by experience at first as a newspaper reporter and, during the last three decades, as a press officer in the Swedish Foreign Ministry and abroad. Further, it is important to me to make it clear that, although you will undoubtedly be reminded of recent American debates on relations between the government and the press, I do not intend to interfere in this struggle. Obviously, after only five years in Washington I am not in a position to judge the continuous mutual accusations between the administration and the press.

Cecil Day Lewis, a British poet and an Oxford professor of literature, is known to a broader public as Nicholas Blake, the author of a series of crime novels. During World War II he headed one of the departments of the Ministry of Information in London. One of his novels is—if my memory does not mislead me—a spy story written as if from within the ministry. The narrative is opened by a discussion between two senior officers on the question of which one of two candidates to employ for a vacant press information job, one an advertising expert and the other one a poet. The department chief, who obviously is the author's *alter ego* and expresses his views, is inclined to prefer the poet to the advertising man on the ground that *poets usually believe in what they say.*

I am not prepared to verify the author's judgment of poets' and ad men's relative honesty. I would not be surprised if there were honest ad people as well as dishonest poets—but this is not

15

the point. Nicholas Blake has in my opinion expressed here a vital basic rule for all governmental information activities in relation to the press: persuading and convincing slogans must never be substituted for truth. In the choice between a poet with a passion for truth and an ever-so-brilliant ad man to whom sales results are more important than verity, you should always choose the poet as your spokesman to the press. I will try to explain why.

When governments of democratic states tell news media (and through them the general public) about their problems, plans, and achievements, the public and the press like to think that the main reason for this is an acceptance of the people's right to know. And of course, in principle that is so. A government that does not agree to freedom of information or freedom of the press as a basic element in the relations between those governing and those governed thereby proves itself a nondemocratic regime, as far as principles are concerned.

Often, however, there is considerable difference between theory and practice. Governments usually do not need any persuasion to give out information that is likely to improve the government's image and appeal to the voters; but as soon as attractive results of this kind seem doubtful, or involve a foreseeable loss of popularity, the willingness of governments to satisfy the people's right to know shows a sudden decline or total disappearance. This natural and human characteristic that governments share with all of us—that we like information much better when it hurts our opponents than when it hurts us—leads governments into the temptation of being generous with the first kind of information and a little more abstemious with the other kind. This is the first and rather innocent step on the dangerous road of managing the news.

This road can be fateful to governments. Theoretically they love freedom of the press for its own sake. In practice they love it exactly as much as they can use it for promoting their own purposes. It seems favorable to government that the public and the press (used here in its wide meaning of news media) get the information suited to influence them in accordance with the government's wishes. So far everything is all right, but then many governments land in a pitfall by holding back information that does not seem advantageous. Very few governments, if any, are so skilled in the information field that they can manage, in the long run, to suppress or gild unfavorable news and yet keep the full confidence of press and people.

At the far end of this road waits the catastrophic abyss where the government completely loses its credibility. This means a failure. It means that the government has thrown away exactly what its information policy was expected to capture, the trust of the people, an indispensable condition of good democratic leadership. The more essential an authoritative and efficient leadership is to a nation, as in times of crisis, the more necessary to the government is the credence of the people. Churchill's unparalleled disclosures to the British people of even very disquieting news during World War II have already set a classic example of the vital importance of uncompromising honesty as a means by which the leader wins the reliance of the people. A nation that knows beyond any doubt that it is given the truth will stand bad news much better than if it does not know what to believe.

The interests of the government and those of the press are in reality usually more opposed to each other than necessary. This opposition is more dramatic in some democratic countries than in others. In the U.S. there seems to be a rather sharp contrast in this field. I do not know who is responsible for this, the administration or the press, but I would suggest it is both of them. It was very interesting to meet this antagonism of views in the book *The Press in Washington,* published in 1966 and containing lectures at the American University by 16 prominent newsmen. Among those 16, Marvin Kalb, Columbia Broadcasting System's chief diplomatic correspondent, seems to me as the most radical spokesman of the public's right to know. On the other front is Richard Fryklund, at that time a Pentagon reporter with the *Washington Evening Star.* As an efficient newsman, Fryklund of course has a full understanding of the public's right to know, but at the same time he strongly defends classification and management of news as a means of keeping such things secret as cannot be told to the enemy. (Fryklund was recently appointed to a position in the office of the Assistant Secretary of Defense for Public Affairs.)

Marvin Kalb is fundamentally and profoundly skeptical of

every pronouncement from the State Department. The task of the Assistant Secretary of State for Public Affairs is, in Kalb's eyes, to protect the administration from premature news reports and from news "that he feels to be detrimental to the interests of the U.S., as he [the Assistant Secretary] interprets them." Kalb's conclusion seems to be that the reporter should refrain from publication only if the administration can convince him that the news would be detrimental to the nation's interests as he himself interprets those interests. As far as I can see, however, he has not in his article solved the dilemma: how can the reporter without access to the whole story as it appears in the department's secret files be confident that his own judgment on the effects of publication is more reliable than the State Department's?

As a stark contrast to Kalb's far-reaching skepticism of the spokesmen of the State Department, there is Fryklund's surprisingly generous defense of the Defense Department's different ways of concealing or adjusting news. After the Cuban crisis in 1962, Arthur Sylvester, the former Assistant Secretary of Defense for Public Affairs, made a public statement that has ever since then been very much debated and opposed in press circles: a public official has a right to lie for his country. Not even this arouses Fryklund's objections. On the contrary, his comment is: "I think he is right—though I would draw the line a little closer to the truth than he would."

A little later I shall discuss Kalb's and Fryklund's views, as both of them are sharply in conflict with my picture of the ideal governmental spokesman. First I should answer a question from my readers: why do I write so much about the relations between the administration and the press of your own country; did I not sit down to my typewriter to tell you of my activities and experiences as a press officer of one country, Sweden, in relation to the press of another country, the United States?

Yes, I did; but I want to emphasize that a government's policy in relation to its own press and its policy vis-à-vis the foreign press should be one and indivisible. More than once a government may feel tempted to give its own people one explanation and tell quite another story abroad. Sometimes it may prefer to give its own nation the true story while misleading other countries. On other occasions it is unwilling to confess to its countrymen that it has felt obliged to make concessions to another state. A spokesman who is shortsighted enough to try to tell contradictory stories at home and abroad will soon find out that this method is not a successful way of creating confidence and being trusted. Usually he will have to present the facts in different ways to domestic and foreign publics. Should he give way, however, to the unhealthy idea of changing the facts from one version to the other, so that he issues one report that is true and one that is not, he will before long be very much in trouble. Even if he is not truth-loving by nature he will learn without delay that sticking to real facts is the easiest way of telling a consistent story—or he will be well advised to seek another profession.

Of course no government is always prepared to disclose to the public at home and abroad all its decisions, indecisions, and internal divisions, but some governments more than others will appreciate it as an advantage if their peoples do not meet all governmental announcements with disbelief because they are used to being fed lies or half truths. There are governments that are clearly aware that confidence and trust are worth their price. They know that if you want to be relied on, you must now and then give out a little more information than is quite convenient to you.

Let me mention as an example Norway, which was governed by essentially one cabinet for 20 years after the end of World War II. All that time one man served in the Prime Minister's office as Under Secretary for Public Affairs. He was a former newspaper reporter. His main task was to answer the daily stream of questions from the press. In order to prepare him for this difficult job, the Prime Minister let him attend cabinet conferences, councils at which decisions were formally made, as well as more informal meetings at which plans were candidly discussed. In this manner he no doubt got a good deal of insight into matters that the chiefs of departments did not want to see published. This man had a stubborn belief in honesty and straightforwardness, and he told the newspapers the truth and nothing but the truth—not always the *whole* truth but always *only* the truth.

As the years passed, he enjoyed more and more unfaltering confidence from the press of all political parties, from the opposition parties' press as well as the press of the government's party.

Now and then cabinet members were annoyed and let him know it. But his imperturbable answer was: "Any day you tell me that you don't want me in this job any longer I will leave immediately. But as long as I am handling the press affairs I will stick to my policy of as much openness as possible." No one ever wished him away. Everyone saw that the credibility his honesty and candidness had given him with the press was a great asset to the government.

His success as a press officer perhaps was an obstacle to his own career. Probably the cabinet considered him qualified for higher public positions, but obviously felt it could not do without him in the press job.

This man was, in my judgment, the ideal governmental press officer. Naturally he had a dependable basic loyalty to his employer, the cabinet. Without that loyalty it would not have been possible to let him in on all kinds of secrets. However, by acting as a good reporter, eager to give the public as much information and as many correct facts as possible, rather than as a red-tape bureaucrat who feels more secure the more facts he can manage to conceal from the press and the public, he was of the greatest use and value to the press, of course, but also—and this is the point—to the government. This was made possible by his employers' wise realization that it is better to be a little too liberal in giving out information and accept the inconveniences that now and then may follow than to cause a loss of confidence by holding back a little too much.

The most important task of the press officer, as I see it, is to sell this insight to the government. That means that he will have to exert at least as much pressure on his employers as on his clients, the press.

Now I am again ready for Kalb and Fryklund and my objections to parts of their highly interesting articles. Of course I agree with Kalb that no foreign ministry spokesman in any country will ever be able to tell the diplomatic reporters everything they want to know and still keep his job, a fact that often will place him in opposition to the newsmen. I do not, however, agree that his job is to protect the administration from news. On the contrary, all the good press officers with whom I have discussed these problems strongly feel that their main duty is to elicit news from the administration. They know that by stubbornly struggling and persuading in this respect, they are serving their government in the best way.

Naturally they will never be successful in their efforts if they are not fundamentally loyal to their country and if they are not led by good judgment and a sense of responsibility. The administration and the press in a free country serve different purposes and there will always be a fight between the two. "Woe befalls a country where the police and the press are at peace."

Thus the good press officer is doomed to permanent strife on two fronts: with the administration and with the press.

Just as I agree with Kalb to a large extent, I also agree with Fryklund. Of course many acts have to be classified in every defense department as well as in every department of foreign affairs. Management of news seems to me more dubious. I do not accept it as a method of deceiving the public on purpose, but I must admit that it is impossible to avoid every kind of management. I myself am managing news every time I tell a reporter a story: intentionally or unintentionally I stress certain facts that I find good news while passing over in silence other facts I find insignificant but that the reporter might have found most newsworthy.

I definitely disagree with Fryklund, however, on his defense of Mr. Sylvester's well-known remark about a public official's right to lie for his country, and especially I object to this policy as applied to press officers.

Let me try to make my view clear by giving an example from another field. Suppose that a friend of yours says to you: "I am unhappy that I lied to you about my brother but I was taken unaware and didn't find the right words. A straight answer would have made my brother innocently suspect of theft." All of us will be prepared to forgive the man for his lie because of his apparent dislike of lying and of the extenuating circumstances; but suppose instead that your friend had said to you before you had asked your question: "When asked about my family I claim the right of lying." That is quite another thing, and you will never trust what he tells you about his family.

I guess that Mr. Sylvester's declaration should be put on a par with the first case above. It was an excuse for a statement made under extenuating circumstances and with patriotic intent. A press officer who would seriously announce as his policy that he will feel free to lie whenever he deems it necessary would be of no use as a press agent because no one would ever know when he was telling the truth.

Look for a moment at the advertising business. More and more it is turning over from illusory promises to honest descriptions of goods as better suited to win the customers' goodwill. Unfortunately there are still many cheap and unscrupulous public relations activities going on, deceiving the ignorant part of the public. However, customers of press attachés are reporters and news commentators; they belong to the intelligent and knowledgeable part of the public, and a deceitful approach to that kind of client is doomed to failure.

This may seem too extensive an introduction in order to come to a rather plain and self-evident ground rule for press officers: you cannot always be completely candid, but *what you say should always be unfailingly true*. There are always moral reasons for that, and even if some politicians and bureaucrats should think otherwise there is no need of defense of a moral behavior in an activity whose foundation is confidence and trust. Truth is very much to be recommended for tactical reasons, in any case, as long as you are looking forward to staying on in the job. Because in this profession the temptations of now and then temporarily abandoning the path of truth are unusually strong, and because many newsmen think that more or less all press officers give way to pressures of this kind, I have meant in all sincerity to try to present the important role of honesty in the information officer's relations to the press.

I hope to have given you the ideological background of my actual activities as a counselor for press affairs at our embassy in Washington. To a small country like mine (not in area but in population) there are quite a few obvious grounds for wishing to improve your nation's knowledge of us.

Most Americans have a vague and superficial idea of a wintry little European country up under the north pole, with a population that is ambitious and highly qualified in some fields but rather peculiar and irresponsible in other areas. Many people look at our social security as something frightening that makes us so tired and unhappy that we commit suicide with record speed; at our morals as low—pleasurably low some tourists seem to hope until they return in deepest disappointment, looking for comfort in their own country; and at our political system as dangerously close to communism.

We may be prejudiced but we don't agree to this image. We would very much like to substitute real knowledge for these rather dull clichés. For political, cultural, and economic reasons we want the people of the world and not least of this great nation to have a somewhat more realistic picture of Sweden.

How do you change a nation's image of another nation? Many people at home seem to think that would be easy. As taxpayers they give us our pay—and want to know, what do we do all the time? Why don't we see to it that the name of Sweden shines out in neon splendor all over the world? I must admit that I still have to discover how that marvelous trick is done, and at almost no cost at all. I did not start working this miracle my first day here in Washington, and I have not managed it yet, five years later.

What do I do? I try to get in personal contact with American newspapermen, mainly here in Washington, but also to some degree in other parts of the country. A few of these relationships have developed into real friendship, and note, please, that I do not use the word friend in that rather light and easygoing manner you often hear it used in this country. My friends bring me in touch with their friends in the press. We discuss, of course, like all other people in this capital, current American politics, and have an exciting time. They try to help me understand what I read in the newspaper that morning.

It is a fascinating job, and sometimes I feel almost ashamed of being paid for having so much fun. How can my employers, the Swedish government, let me spend much of my time in this way instead of putting up neon signs in the skies? It is because from their point of view my time spent with American reporters has a quite serious purpose: establishing a network of trustful relations. I can depend on the information and advice I get from my American friends and there is a chance that a few of them will be aware that I try, to the best of my ability, to give them correct and honest information about my country whenever they want it. I think these channels of information are helpful and essential to our purpose of creating a correct image of our country.

Reporters whom I do not know probably often take it for granted that as a paid propagandist I will give them a beautified picture of my country. Without the personal relationship and its support of credibility, a foreign embassy officer who approaches a newspaper often finds to his disappointment that his story is met by skepticism as official propaganda whose relationship to reality is considered as highly suspicious.

How do we get our message to the American public through the news media? I will be glad to tell you a little about what I believe I have learned in this field.

In the first place, we should not imagine that the American press day after day is starving for news from Sweden. Should we call for the attention of the press all the time it would get tired of us. It is so much more important for us to be prepared and on the alert as soon as Sweden is drawn into the limelight and one aspect or another of my country, perhaps for a few hours or days, attracts the interest of the American press. This usually arrives in one of two ways: either something happens in Sweden that seems interesting, or Sweden turns out to be a useful argument pro or con in the domestic political debate in this country. In the first case we have to call or cable Stockholm for a briefing on the matter if they have not anticipated the interest from the American press and given us information in advance. In the latter case we usually can to some degree foresee the American demand and be prepared. It was not difficult to know that the current American administration's drive for Medicare, old age pension, and antipoverty reforms would bring about interest among Americans, liberals as well as conservatives, in our experiences in the corresponding areas. And I need not tell you that without hesitation we give information to opponents of these reforms as well as to supporters.

Now and then we submissively must accept the fact that what we thought to be a genuine interest in Swedish policy and in our ways of living is instead a need for arguments in domestic American political struggle. A few years ago I was chatting idly at the luncheon table with an American friend, a reporter, when I remembered a story about Swedish welfare that had recently been published by his magazine. I told him in a friendly way that I did not mind the criticism but that I was disappointed to see how the reporter, who knew better and was familiar with Sweden, had distorted the whole thing by stressing all negative aspects and passing over the positive ones in silence. A little to my surprise my friend answered in the same relaxed manner: "Had you expected us to recommend the Swedish system? You know we are conservative and definitely opposed to the President's welfare program." What mattered was not how things were in Sweden but how they did not want them to be in the United States.

In line with what I have said earlier about the importance of confident relations with the press, I think we press officers should try to get in direct touch with the news media as much as possible without any intermediaries. Of course there can be situations when this is impossible and you need to hire a public relations agent; but then you lose some pleasure and some experience and above all you miss one step in your endeavor to lay the basis of a trustful relationship with the press.

How should you react when you meet unfriendly attitudes from American newspapers and what can you do to correct false impressions? First, do not get angry; try to keep your temper. In some cases there is not much you can do. For example, before next issue of the newspaper goes to print you cannot usually convert the editor from his convinced opposition to social welfare and have him decide to present the Swedish system in a manner you yourself will find fair. Of course you should not question the honesty of his opinions or try to press his convictions. One day perhaps you will find a natural opportunity to get your message through.

One of the worst setbacks the reputation of Sweden's social welfare ever had in the United States was the effect of remarks by President Eisenhower at a breakfast at the Republican Convention in Chicago in 1960, when he argued against this kind of reform with reference to the alleged rising suicide rate and low morals in a fairly friendly European country following a tremendous socialistic operation (no one doubted that he had Sweden in mind). This verdict got immense publicity all over the country. I remember how a little later in that year—this was before my arrival in Washington—I asked my predecessor here what they did to meet this statement, completely wrong as it is. (Our suicide rate is relatively high and has been for many decades. The cause of this phenomenon is unclear but is obviously not the welfare reforms). He answered that they could do nothing. They could as well have tried to stop the waves in the ocean. The Democrats, however, did not remain silent. Since they had the opposite view on the matter, Sweden was used by them as an argument for welfare legislation and the intensity of their campaign was so great, and it was so eloquently in favor of Sweden, that our balance sheet showed a good net profit to Sweden's image in the United States—I am still quoting my predecessor.

This nice story is still not finished. It has one or two more points. When the American press after the President's speech asked the acting head of the Swedish Embassy if the President could have been thinking of Sweden, he answered in undisturbed good temper: "He couldn't have been talking about Sweden because he said a 'fairly friendly' country, and Sweden is a *very* friendly one" (*New York Times,* July 29, 1960). That is how to do it.

President Eisenhower's use of Sweden in his breakfast remarks was not very popular in my country. When the heat waves of the election campaign had blown away, Mr. Eisenhower visited Sweden. There he apologized in public for his mistake in such a charming and engaging way that he was immediately, completely, and forever forgiven.

Now and then misunderstandings are caused by differences in the use of words. Some absurd ideas in this country about Sweden are initiated by the word "socialism," which many Americans tend to identify almost with communism. That explains some of the rather stunning questions we sometimes get about our country. Sweden's freedom of the press and other products from the printing press are more safeguarded by law than in any country I know of. It is a very essential part of our constitution. With this in mind you will forgive me my stupefaction when I was asked by a friendly and well-educated American at a pleasant

Swedish-American conference: "Tell me, are there any nongovernment-owned newspapers in your country?"

A few years ago, before Norway's labor government resigned, a Norwegian friend here in Washington told me something that clearly demonstrated the importance of care in the use of words. You will not get the point of this story if you do not know that the Norwegian name of its labor party in English translation is simply "The Norwegian Labor Party," while the exactly corresponding party in my country is called "Sweden's Social-Democratic Labor Party," or, briefly, "The Social-Democrats." The Norwegian disclosed that Americans in contact with him and his colleagues frequently saw a substantial difference between the Swedish and the Norwegian political systems. When told that the difference was practically nonexistent, the Americans insisted, declaring that Sweden had a socialist government and Norway a labor government.

Swedish issues that especially attract interest from the American political press are labor–management relations and social welfare policy.

At the end of my account I find that with typical egotism I have used up my time writing about our job as if it were a one-man theater. I am only one of the cogs in the machinery. At the embassy we have a cultural attaché, Mrs. Ingrid Arvidsson, whose regular job is to be a book reviewer and a poet (one of those persons who, according to Nicholas Blake, believe in what they say); an information officer, Lars Karlström, First Secretary of the embassy; and a few more in the information field. In New York there is a Swedish Information Service, headed by Allan Kastrup and Anders H. Pers, the latter a son of the author of *The Swedish Press*. Of course we try many ways of approach directly to the public: exhibitions of art and of products, films, lectures, concerts, and so on. All these information activities take place under the personal leadership of Sweden's Ambassador to the United States, Hubert de Besche.

Finally, I have a little confession. I have been dwelling so much on truth and confidence that I may have given you the impression of claiming to be some kind of expert in that field. I am not. It is easy to be honest when you are confident that the product you are selling is one of good quality. The salesman who is offering you a really good car can generously admit that the ashtray could have been better located. The seller of a poor car will have a much tougher time being honest.

We who are selling Sweden usually find it rather easy to be candid.

3

The Fight against Misunderstanding

FRANCISCO J. LARA, DIRECTOR
INSTITUTE OF INFORMATION AND CULTURE
EMBASSY OF VENEZUELA

FRANCISCO J. LARA was born in Venezuela and educated at the Colegio Nacional de Varones in San Cristobal. He emigrated to the United States in 1918 and worked for American export firms in Colombia, Venezuela, and Central America.

Mr. Lara began his writing career in 1935, when he was hired by the New York office of Metro-Goldwyn-Mayer to do publicity work. In 1940 he joined the Latin American division of the National Broadcasting Company to write and edit radio programs for shortwave broadcasts. He was supervisor of the Latin American division during the last years of World War II.

When NBC discontinued shortwave broadcasts at the end of the war, he went to work for the Spanish-language newspaper *Diario de Nueva York* as a news and feature writer.

He joined the Venezuelan Embassy in 1950 as director of the Institute of Information and Culture and editor of *Venezuela Up-to-Date,* the embassy publication. He lives in Washington with his wife and has a married daughter living in Madison, New Jersey, a married son in Klamath Falls, Oregon, and a son at the University of Maryland.

SOMEWHAT like Don Quixote, who devoted his life to correcting misdeeds, the cultural attachés and information directors of Washington embassies devote their working hours to correcting misconceptions and misunderstandings about their countries.

These misconceptions and misunderstandings prevail in the United States particularly as regards the Latin American republics, for it is said the people here will do everything for Latin America except to read about it.

Why? The countries to the south of us became independent from Spain some 50 years after the United States became independent from England, but while the United States was developing rapidly and in peace Latin American countries wasted a century in political fights provoked by their leaders' greed for power, to the detriment of their normal growth. Thus they gained the reputation of being politically immature groups of natives unfit to govern themselves. The people of the United States heard nothing but disparaging reports about the Latin Americans and found no reason for paying much attention to them.

Even today, when conditions have greatly changed for the better, many visiting U.S. correspondents, who seem to specialize in bad news, report only the dark side of the picture. Fortunately, others are beginning to realize there is also a bright side, and their dispatches are more realistic.

As the Latin American nations come of age, give themselves constitutional and democratic governments, and substitute order for turmoil, a gratifying curiosity about them is arising in this country—an evident interest in learning more about their doings. Yet too many people still think of Latin America as a vast, steaming jungle full of insects, snakes, and ferocious beasts, peopled by half-naked, miserable Indians.

Here are a few examples: a lady in the Midwest writes that she wants to visit Venezuela but is afraid to go because she has been told the country is teeming with scorpions. A friend of mine met a girl in Washington who, learning that he was from Venezuela, invited him to her house, "and be sure to wear your native dress with feathers and all." A mason in New England says he has been informed there are no men of his trade in Venezuela; he is willing to take a chance and work there, provided he is paid a specified wage, plus traveling expenses, board, and lodging. A lady tells my wife she and her husband are going to Central America and plan to stop at Venezuela.

At the Embassy of Venezuela, thousands of letters come every year asking for all kinds of information on Venezuela. Most of them are from schoolchildren, and nearly all ask the same questions: How do the people live? What do they eat? How do they dress? How do they make a living? And they usually ask also for a picture of the national dress. Surely, other embassies receive similar requests. Venezuelan students in American colleges beg the embassy for literature, films, and slides "to show our fellow students we are not so behind the times as they think."

Here is where the cultural attachés and information directors come in. Patiently and clearly, they must enlighten the questioners. All Latin American countries, except Uruguay, Argentina, and southern Chile, are in the tropics, and certainly, most of them are still covered with dense jungles. But no one lives in the jungle, and as the population grows and more land is needed for farming, the jungle is pushed back.

Temperatures vary according to altitude above sea level, from hot in the lowlands to freezing in the upper reaches of the Andes mountains, and are more or less constant all year, whether in the dry season or the rainy season. Temperatures do not change with the seasons as in the Temperate Zone.

As for Indians, only Mexico, Guatemala, Ecuador, Peru, and Bolivia have considerable Indian populations. Other Latin American countries have small Indian groups, and still others have none at all. The Indian population of Venezuela, for instance, hardly exceeds 100,000.

Scorpions and other insects abound in the jungle, to be sure, along with poisonous snakes and animals of the cat family, but if the lady who is afraid of scorpions were to go to Venezuela, the chances are that she would not see one.

In all Latin American countries, and even in different regions of the same country, women, in particular, wear colorful dresses at special occasions. Everyday clothing, however, is much like the so-called Western clothing we all wear, light in warm climates and heavy in cold climates.

When answering schoolchildren's questions, we are aware our replies may disappoint some of them, for instead of descriptions of a quaint way of life we must tell them that Latin Americans live, dress, eat, and work much as we do here. In the matter of food, some countries have their own native dishes—*tamales* in Mexico, *hallacas* in Venezuela, *cebiche* in Ecuador, *pastel de choclo* in Chile, *churrasco* in Argentina, but outside of these special foods, "standard" food is the daily diet.

As far as Venezuela is concerned, our embassy in Washington makes available as much information as possible by means of fact sheets, statistical data, folders, posters, slides, and a magazine, *Venezuela Up-to-Date,* which reports every important event and has been published for the last 17 years for free distribution to libraries, schools and colleges, teachers, business concerns, and private individuals. We are happy to say that libraries use it as a reference source and teachers as a textbook of contemporary history.

Our embassy's Institute of Information and Culture organizes occasional art exhibitions and entertains an average of three student groups every week. Regrettably, the request for speakers cannot be met every time, although the Ambassador delivers lectures at colleges or before civic organizations whenever he can spare the time. Other embassies have similar or even better services; some also publish magazines and most print periodical newsletters.

The ultimate reason for all these efforts is, of course, that nations, like individuals, want other people to have the best opinion of them. In the case of the Latin American countries the immediate reason is not merely the wish to be better known, but to prove that they are no longer the backward, disorderly peoples of a half-century ago, but nations under different degrees of development, with responsible governments intent on improving the condition of the masses. The retrogression of Cuba under Fidel Castro has shown them that advancement can only be attained by practicing true democracy and avoiding communism. Moreover, without their own financial means to develop the continent's vast natural resources, they want to attract investment capital, technical assistance, and the tourist dollar, and these can only come from the United States.

Ignorance and misunderstandings are not limited to the American public regarding Latin America; it appears also among Latin Americans regarding the United States, despite the torrent of literature, movies, news, and video programs pouring constantly into their countries. The picture of the arrogant and disdainful *gringo* has not been fully eradicated from the minds of many Latin Americans.

And it must be said the United States is doing more to uproot this prejudice than the Latin Americans are doing to improve their image in the eyes of North Americans. The U. S. Department of State frequently sponsors tours for Latin American professionals, newspapermen, and students in the United States, as well as student-exchange programs such as the American Field Service programs. The U. S. Department of Health, Education and Welfare also carries out a student-exchange program. Incidentally, the boys and girls of the Peace Corps, in addition to their worthy work, have unknowingly created more goodwill toward the United States in Latin America than any other effort in that direction. Earning low salaries, they live in poor city sectors they want to help and, of necessity, mix with the common people. They are looked on with suspicion at first, but after they have proved they mean well the suspicion turns into admiration and cooperation.

Venezuela once in a while invites U.S. newpaper correspondents, public officials, students, and artists to visit the country, and probably other Latin American countries do likewise. Venezuela also participates in the exchange of farm boys to work on farms in one another's countries. Without question, these efforts are bound to do much good, and obviously their effect would be greater if they were undertaken more frequently and to a larger extent. This applies to all other Latin American countries.

Efforts should be intensified to show the world the progress made in education, sanitation, social welfare, industrialization, housing, road building, orderly government. What these countries have accomplished, in spite of all that remains to be done, will be a revelation to many people.

Meanwhile, the job of dispelling wrong ideas must go on and on day after day, for it is doubtful the time will come when we can say: Now that everybody understands everybody, we can go home and rest.

4

Building the Image of a New Nation

L. F. KAEMBA
INFORMATION ATTACHÉ
EMBASSY OF THE REPUBLIC OF ZAMBIA

L AXON FRED KAEMBA began his communications career as a reporter for one of the government publications of Zambia in 1957, when it was still a British protectorate known to the world as Northern Rhodesia. In 1962 he undertook intensive research in African languages at the School of Oriental and African Studies, London University. While in England he reported for the *Bristol Evening Post*.

Mr. Kaemba returned to Zambia in 1964 as editor of a government newspaper, *Lyashi* (now called *Imbila*). In early 1965 he was appointed Information Attaché to the Embassy of the Republic of Zambia in Washington.

THE basic task of a press counselor in an embassy is to project the true image of his country. In some embassies he is referred to as information attaché, press attaché, or press counselor. In this article I shall refer to this officer as Information Attaché, for this is what I am called in my embassy. Of course, if you called me press attaché or press counselor I would still answer; it is only a matter of titles.

The Information Attaché is, in most cases, seconded to the Foreign Service from the Ministry of Information. In his endeavor to publicize his country he must approach the various avenues to the public with maximum effectiveness. He cannot be effective if his work is not well planned. What then does he do to ensure maximum success?

The Information Attaché knows very well that he cannot succeed in his task without the help and cooperation of other people. It is important therefore that when he takes up his duties it must be his first duty to find these indispensable elements of the public—the representatives of all major media in the country where he is stationed. He should have contacts with national daily and weekly newspapers, specialist publications, broadcasting and television organizations, and the various divisions of the information department of the host government.

For example, I have to work at times with the Voice of America. I may find it necessary to broadcast to Zambia and explain something that has taken place at the United Nations, perhaps in reference to the Zambian economic mission or within the Security Council. I pick up a phone and call someone with whom I have previously made contact at VOA and say, "At such and such a time can you let me broadcast to Zambia?" Obviously, the time to make contacts for this sort of cooperation is early, long before the need arises.

In order to establish such contacts, to comprehend the type of material they require and how it should be presented to ensure the best chance of publication, the Information Attaché will need to keep himself well informed. This is very important. He bears the burden of establishing the integrity of both his government and himself in the eyes of the media.

The Information Attaché deals with extremely sensitive elements of the public. He can be easily understood or misunderstood. It is true that although certain individuals from the press are sincere to their profession, others are not. They allow personal attitudes to influence their work at the risk of their journalistic integrity.

Whatever the case may be, the Information Attaché is supposed to be as helpful as possible. He should not issue untruthful or biased material; the press has its own sources of information and will quickly discover the truth. If the Information Attaché furnishes false information to the press, the confidence he has been able to create will be irretrievably destroyed. Obviously, there could be no worse disservice to his government and himself than the loss of respect among the people with whom he is dealing.

The Information Attaché therefore tries to avoid any embarrassing situation with anybody anywhere. He expurgates his material before it is sent out. In addition, the Head of his Mission checks and double checks the material for precision and clarity before the final product is released.

In order to help the American press and ultimately the American public to know and understand the views of his government, the Information Attaché prepares press releases, talks to press representatives on the telephone, or sometimes in person at parties, and sends them all available information material. Some of the press organizations are ill-informed about new nations like Zambia. Consequently, what the public—which is largely dependent on what is printed in papers and what is said on the radio and television—does not know about these new nations can be shocking and dangerous. The cause for this profound ignorance is their source of information—the press. It is important, therefore, to feed the press with as much accurate material as possible so that they, in turn, can pass it on to the public.

We all know how useful the press can be in disseminating information. We also know how destructive it can be if it has no access to correct and full facts. That is why I insist that if we succeed in educating the press, we shall have automatically achieved remarkable success in educating the public.

Early in 1967, for example, the President of Zambia issued a statement agreeing to cooperate in economic sanctions against Rhodesia. About 10 days later a member of the American press wrote his own version of this story, saying Zambia had "refused" to cooperate in the sanctions. I had only to send a copy of the speech made before the story was written. Most newsmen are very cooperative when you give them the facts.

Sometimes the press may issue hostile statements about a country represented by an Information Attaché. This is a situation that cannot be rectified by a counter-hostile approach. This is a serious crisis and it is incumbent on the Information Attaché to exercise utmost humility in writing to the press concerned and providing the true facts. Normally editors and other press representatives are reasonable people. They will listen and make the necessary adjustments.

There are times when matters get out of hand. At this point it becomes necessary for the Head of the Mission to issue a statement. He does this in two ways: by calling a press conference or by sending out press statements to all major media. In both cases it is the Information Attaché who coordinates the activities. He arranges the time and place for the meeting to take place or issues a press release on what his Head of the Mission wants the press and the public to know. This is especially necessary in time of crisis, when chances of misunderstanding are greater.

One of the things emphasized in journalism is that a person should have a "nose for news," but it is my conviction that, coupled with this quality, a successful journalist should possess tact to enable him to pursue any news clues successfully. Some reporters mislay tact in the wave of irresistable emotion and excitement. Others do not have trustworthy or reliable sources. Also, when a reporter cannot squeeze anything worth a filler out of his source he sometimes becomes desperate. The only way he sees out of this predicament is to resort to misguided imagination, which is very dangerous. This is the beginning of what is often attacked in the press as distortion and misrepresentation of facts.

It is this type of reporting that alarms an Information Attaché. Probably I should say this type of reporting gives him work to do.

The Information Attaché tries as much as possible to keep abreast with events in his home country. The embassy subscribes to home newspapers. He also receives press releases and telegrams from his home country. Tickers have proved very useful in following daily events all over the world, and they have become a great asset to most foreign representatives.

The Information Attaché is the adviser to the Head of the Mission on all matters pertaining to public relations and information. He acts as liaison link between the media organizations and all officials and nationals who visit the United States from his home country. He travels the length and breadth of the United States, lecturing to schools and organizations; his talks and lectures are illustrated by films. While on tours he makes contacts with the press in each state. Whatever he does, he never forgets contacts; he must make a point of meeting the press and television media people in every area.

Most of the Information Attachés are trained in audiovisual presentation. They assist trade representatives with displays at trade fairs and other important promotional shows.

While engulfed in all this work, the Information Attaché attends to all ordinary requests for information on his country. He receives letters from professors and lecturers and from university, high-school, and elementary-school students. From such requests he ascertains the kind of publication for which a demand exists and that could be prepared by his department in his home country. In this way it is possible to stock material to fulfill almost every request.

There is only one request that I have been consistently unable to fulfill. During my stay in Washington I have received many letters asking for a recipe for our national food. We do have a national dish. It is mush—a thick porridge—eaten with relish; but we have many different types of relish, cooked in many different ways. This is something I have been unable to get across.

Requests for a copy of the national recipe have come to my office many, many times in the past two years, but I shall probably go home at the end of my tour of duty without having filled the requests to the satisfaction of the people writing in.

Through personal contacts, talks, lectures, films, slides, and distribution of literature, people gradually begin to feel the existence of a new and small nation like Zambia. Letters from all elements of the public have been particularly enlightening. They have given me a vivid idea of how much and what people in the United States know about my country. I was amused when I received a letter from a college student who wanted to know "how Africans in Zambia and other African countries manage to live with lions and snakes in the same houses."

Nobody can blame this college student for such ignorance. He expressed feelings that have been instilled in him by those who claim to possess expert knowledge on Africa. I have yet to meet an American student who has been exposed to true facts about some of these things. So far, their knowledge and that of the public as a whole can only be described as pathetic. I told this student that I had never seen a lion until I went to a zoo in Britain in 1964. I hope I was able to make a meaningful impression on him.

Because of such encounters I am inclined to think that the prime remedy is to correct the source of information, and this is exactly what every Information Attaché is striving to do. I am pleased to state that I have found most reporters throughout the United States and Canada willing to learn the truth. They are making use of every facility available at the embassies and missions. They never put out any statement without checking with the embassy representatives concerned.

The Information Attaché is usually a very busy man. He arranges conferences and interviews for his Head of Mission and produces a newsletter for distribution to his nationals and to the American public. In embassies where there is a staff shortage he also assumes the responsibilities of a cultural officer. These two offices are very similar.

He advises prospective visitors to his country on climate, clothing, food, tourist resorts, and other general information.

The Information Attaché may be alone but never lonely. There are numerous telephone calls, expected and unexpected visitors, and requests. The work is hard and challenging, but at the same time it is rewarding to a conscientious and dedicated officer.

5

How It's Done

A. L. VALENCIA
PRESS COUNSELOR
EMBASSY OF THE PHILIPPINES

A L VALENCIA's "beat" for the last 20 years has been Washington, D.C. During that time he has alternated between being a newspaperman and an information officer serving five Philippine Presidents. He is now a Special Assistant to President Ferdinand E. Marcos and is assigned to the Philippine Embassy as Press Counselor.

Before coming to Washington, Mr. Valencia was news editor of the Manila bureau of the Associated Press. He was a war correspondent attached to General Douglas MacArthur's headquarters during the early stages of World War II. After the fall of Manila he joined the Filipino underground and was imprisoned twice by the Japanese military police. Following the liberation he worked as reporter and news editor of *Free Philippines,* a newspaper published by the U.S. Office of War Information.

Mr. Valencia has retired from government service three times, but has been pressed back into service each time. When he is not working for the government he serves as Washington correspondent for Manila newspapers. His byline has appeared in all of Manila's six major dailies.

THERE is an old saying that the job of a diplomat is to lie for his country. Although I do not know that I myself would accept that as necessarily true, I suppose one could, if cynically inclined, define the job of the Press Counselor as lying to the press for one's country.

If that were the whole story, of course, I could end right there. It is not. It is much more complex than that.

Obviously, one of the main roles a Press Counselor has to fill is that of being a public relations officer for his country in the capital to which he is accredited. But another task that is quite as important is that of keeping his superiors—his ambassador, foreign office, and government—informed about press reactions to developments at home as they are reported here.

He can be called on to predict what the various editorial writers, columnists and opinion-makers of the press, radio, and television in the United States are likely to say if his government does this or that. He can also be expected to advise on whether it matters what certain commentators think—which candidly means he has to judge whether so-and-so currently cuts any ice in the White House.

Without wishing to be unkind, I must say that this matter has been somewhat simplified of late. At least, if one believes what one reads, it would seem that rather few of my friends are "in" at the moment; but doubtless this is only a passing phase. Suffice it to say I keep my ears open for gossip about who is up and who is down at any given moment on Washington's merry-go-round.

I have been asked to explain how a person in my position sets about reaching the American press. A simple and truthful answer is: I reach for the telephone. I do not think that is what you want to know, however, so I will explain further.

There are all sorts of ways of setting about my task, just as there are of selling soap or car rental services. Some countries spend vast amounts on it. The British Information Services, for example, are said to cost a million dollars a year in the United States alone.

Some countries actually contract out: for example, the New York public relations firm of Hill & Knowlton handles Saudi Arabia's press relations entirely—right down to selecting the newsmen to be invited to a private background press conference with King Faisal when he was last here.

It is not for me to say whether this is a good idea. My Saudi friends must think so, and it is their affair. I did wonder about it, however, when one of the favored few—an old colleague of mine who was bidden to the King's suite at the Waldorf that summer— remarked to me bitterly afterwards, "He didn't give us each a watch." He was annoyed about it. Apparently the legend that Saudi monarchs invariably bestow gold wristwatches on their journalistic interviewers is without foundation. I think a smart press counselor would have tipped the boys off about that in advance—so as to avoid disappointment.

Many countries among the 116 with embassies in Washington put out elaborate literature, pamphlets, brochures, and news-letters, and mail them to all the correspondents and editors in town. I am not myself entirely convinced that this pays. It is easy to overdo it; then stories tend to be ignored and wind up with other junk mail in so many wastebaskets.

On the other hand, I do think it useful to keep facts and figures on file and up to date at all times so as to be ready to supply current data about my country to those who are interested or whom I want to interest. The essential thing, surely, is to be available to the press and alert to its needs.

Now, of course, the Philippines is rather a special case as far as her relations with the United States is concerned. Frankly, because of this I sometimes feel there is a tendency on both our parts to take one another for granted. This in the long run may be dangerous because a generation is inevitably growing up in both countries that shares no common memories—to whom Bataan means nothing, for example—and therefore no ties.

Up to the present, however, I would say that because of this— our long past association with the United States—the main problem that faces me as Press Counselor in Washington is not how to deal with a hostile press, but rather how to get the American press to notice us.

I am sure that the best way to do this is by personal contacts. And happily for me it is both my business and pleasure to know personally most of the top journalists in Washington. That I was a working newsman myself with the Associated Press helped a lot, of course, because I can see how things look from both sides (it has sometimes struck me that there must be about as many frustrated journalists in diplomatic ranks as frustrated diplomats among journalists, and it might be fun if for an experiment they could all switch for a spell).

When false impressions crop up, misunderstandings in the press—which really is a euphemism for bits of news that we do not like, either because they are wrong, exaggerated, distorted, or all three, or because we wish they were—it is, of course, the Press Counselor's job to try to fix matters up. He can do this by issuing a flat denial, over the Ambassador's signature or his own. He may write a letter to the editor of the paper that carried the offending story, in an effort to set the record straight. I must say, however, that in many cases it is better to ignore these things; to make a great fuss often makes a mountain out of a molehill.

I personally find it more effective to persuade an editor or a reporter who has written something hurtful about us that there is another side to the story, rather than to flatly contradict him. After all, few Americans are malicious about us when we come right down to it, and there is not much that could be done about those who may be deliberately so.

It has been my experience that the American press generally tries to be fair. Having said that, however, I must admit too that I do not think it pays much attention to us, and also that there is always a tendency to play up abrasive news rather than favorable. But this is true, after all, about much of your domestic news selection.

For example, if anyone in Manila criticizes U.S. policy in Vietnam, there will be a few paragraphs about it in the *Washington Post*. But it may surprise you to know that when we sent two battalions of combat engineers to Vietnam last year, it was hardly mentioned anywhere. In the *New York Times* it merited a brief, single-column story, below the fold on an inside page.

On the other hand, of course, we did enjoy a very good press when President Marcos and his wife came over on their state visit in 1966. Unquestionably the fact that our President and his wife are handsome and photogenic helped in this. His fine war record and her beauty made them a PR man's dream. However, he also had things to say that impressed people here; he discussed an awakening, resurgent mood in free Asia.

Naturally, before he came I saw to it that every columnist, editor, and diplomatic correspondent in the country was fully briefed about him, his record, and his recent pronouncements on political affairs. I was careful to be factual and not dress up this material because (a) frankly, it was unnecessary, and (b) I think it is usually counterproductive to go in for exaggerated embroidery in these cases.

The most important thing, therefore, was to let your opinion-makers know something about my President and what he stood for—and what he was therefore likely to talk about when he met President Johnson—before he arrived here, in such a way as to arouse their interest.

Perhaps more important, though, it was my duty to assess in advance for him what kind of reaction he could expect from the American press when he got here and the type of question he could expect to be asked at press conferences, and generally to outline the attitudes toward and preconceptions about the Philippines that he would encounter here. Obviously I could not do this without hinting at subjects to avoid and others to emphasize, but I must insist that in the final analysis, it is not the function of a counselor to do more than counsel.

To sum up: I do not think there is or should be any great mystery about what a Press Counselor does in any embassy. His is a liaison job. Indeed, the function of diplomacy itself nowadays is largely to provide liaison between governments, especially in a time when it has become the practice for national leaders to get together at "summits" with increasing frequency, rather than to negotiate, still less initiate anything of much moment.

In dealing with the press I always think it wise not to try to fool anybody. Happily I am not required to tell lies anyway, for I am not very good at it. However, there is a little rhyme I learned from an Englishman that I sometimes find myself repeating; I gather it was written by G. K. Chesterton about the British newsman, but it applies as well to the American. It goes:

You cannot bribe or twist
the honest British journalist.
But seeing what the chap will do
unbribed, there is no reason to!

6

The Modern Age
of Spain

JAIME DE URZAIZ
COUNSELOR OF INFORMATION
EMBASSY OF SPAIN

J AIME DE URZAIZ was born in Madrid in 1929 and was educated at the Universities of Madrid and Salamanca. An attorney, he is also a former newsman, having served as an accredited correspondent in Italy for *Diario de Barcelona, Norte de Castilla, Las Provincias, Piel de España,* and Radio Nacional de Barcelona. He has also contributed articles to various Spanish and foreign dailies and magazines.

A member of the Spanish Association of Travel Writers, the Association of Orientalists, the Spanish Center for Public Relations (CENERP), and the Public Relations Society of America (PRSA), he has held the positions of Deputy Director for the Spanish National Tourist Office in Rome, Director of the Spanish National Tourist Office in Milan, and Chief of the Department of Foreign Relations of the Ministry for Information and Tourism in Madrid.

He came to Washington in 1964 with his wife and three daughters, and holds the diplomatic rank of Counselor for Information and Tourism with the Embassy of Spain.

To WRITE of modern Spain in terms of history, which counts the life of nations in centuries rather than in years, would be too broad a subject. Therefore I shall limit myself to some aspects of modern Spain, and more specifically, of contemporary Spain, that is, Spain today.

After a long political "siesta" or nap—during which disorder and disruption brought the nation to her knees—Spain heard the trumpet call of the dramatic and bloody Civil War of 1936 to 1939. Chaos prevailed throughout the nation. The Government of the Republic was incapable of restraining the atavistic or ancestral impulses of the Spaniard, which within only a few years completed the work of national destruction, crowned tragically by the anarchy and the chaos of the Popular Front.

Although the Civil War was historically necessary, I shall not speak about it, for I belong to the generation of those who did not go to war, simply because I was not old enough to fight.

During the years that followed the war Spain underwent the normal changes and convulsions to be expected after the terrific earthquake represented by the civil conflict of 1936.

Thirty years have passed. This is a long time, and Spain has undergone many changes.

First of these was the economic one that amazed economists all over the world; they called it "the Spanish Miracle."

Today the nation's per capita income has jumped to $630, thus passing and leaving behind the ignominious and degrading line that divides the developing nations from the underdeveloped ones. Indeed, during the past 28 years of peace, Spain has rebuilt herself physically and spiritually. The recent referendum held on December 14, 1966, resulted in a 95.90 percent vote by the people in favor of the New Constitutional Law presented by the Chief of State and Government. This was an unprecedented—except for the referendum held in 1947 under similar circumstances—demonstration of unanimity, united thinking, and action on the part of the Spanish people. The majority of those who cast their ballots in the recent referendum—all Spanish males and females over 21 years of age—belong to generations who did not take part in the war. They are the generations of present-day, modern, progressive Spain—a nation that, having behind it a rich historical heritage, now resumes the position it deserves in world affairs.

These are the facts that should be known by all countries, and particularly by you in the United States, as a background for my statements in this chapter in my capacity as Information Counselor.

The task of an information counselor is a many-sided one.

In the first place, he is a public relations man. His primary task is to make his country known, to present its best aspects and the progress achieved in its general development. As we shall see, such objectives are not easy when you are faced with informing a huge nation like the United States.

Another phase of this task, which may be described as a disagreeable one, is to correct the "black legend" that clings to the country to be presented; to correct and refute malicious newspaper articles, prejudiced or partisan books, viewpoints, and politics that in some way may hurt the prestige of the nation. Speaking on the basis of more than three years of hard work in this country, I have been amazed by two principal things: the general unawareness of Americans about Spain, and the fury that those who do know her inject into their discussions of Spanish political matters.

Far from making my task easier, these factors make it difficult.

In line with the first objective described, the Information Department of the Embassy of Spain uses three tools for informing the public. The first is an eight-page illustrated monthly bulletin, known as the *Spanish Newsletter*, which reports outstanding events about our nation in foreign and domestic affairs, religion, economics, tourism, culture, and so forth. The *Spanish Newsletter* includes a special "insert," featuring some subject of current interest, in greater detail. More than 16,000 copies of this publication are distributed in the United States, and even go to Canada and the Far East. We feel that this distribution is almost 100 percent effective because it employs a mailing list of personal requests for the publication. The *Spanish Newsletter* has already proved its effectiveness, and it is interesting to note that, for example, the *New York Times* quotes it frequently as the source of news published in its columns.

Our second medium of information distribution is another eight-page publication entitled *The Week in Spain*. As its name indicates, it is a weekly, and is published by the Spanish Information Service of the Ministry of Information and Tourism in Madrid. This illustrated bulletin gathers from the national and international press outstanding news items of the week. It is published in five languages, and in the United States alone more than 25,000 copies are now distributed, using the same system of a selective mailing list.

The third means we employ to inform is direct communication by letter and by telephone with persons interested in Spain. This work is unassuming and unpretentious but it is extremely effective.

Written requests for data or office interviews are always answered by letter, accompanied by pertinent informational matter. Experience shows that the material distributed in this manner is utilized not only by the person who receives it, but also by various persons in the family or their friends, fellow students, or workers. This procedure is what I call the "spot of oil" method because it imperceptibly spreads and extends its field of influence.

Our public information activity includes the preparation of releases for the American press, radio, and television. Such releases feature news having maximum interest for Spain and for professional newspapermen in general, in view of the impact that they may have on American public opinion.

Finally, in that field of information called public relations, I should mention talks, film showings, the organization of artistic or theatrical events, special motion pictures, concerts, ballet performances, and so on, in which the Information Department of the Embassy of Spain participates to a greater or lesser degree.

This work of making Spain better known in the United States also includes two very important approaches: tourist promotion and advertising.

Today Spain is the leading destination for international tourism. In 1966 Spain received 17,250,000 visitors, that is, more than one-half its actual population. This represents an increase of 21 percent over the previous year. Of the total figure, American tourists accounted for more than 700,000.

That the United States is an important potential tourist source for Spain is shown by the attention the Spanish Ministry of Information and Tourism devotes to it. Today there are five National Spanish Tourist Offices here, located in New York, Chicago, San Francisco, St. Augustine (Florida), and Miami, where an office was recently established. Another office is located in San Juan, capital of the Commonwealth of Puerto Rico.

The tourist offices, completely noncommercial in nature, devote themselves exclusively to encouraging Americans to travel in Spain, and employ personal contact and correspondence. The offices, strategically located in the busiest districts of the cities in which they operate, supply hotel rates, prepare tourist schedules, and suggest the best seasons to visit Spain. At the same time, they work closely with travel agents and travel writers to facilitate their work.

The tourist offices are under the jurisdiction of the Information Counselor of the Embassy, although in practice they work with great independence in their particular field.

They also are responsible for the public relations and advertising campaigns carried out in the United States.

It is interesting to note the growing number of retired Americans who wish to live in Spain, where the cost of living is lower and where they may have a small house by the sea in which they can spend their later years in a more favorable economic situation than their incomes or pensions would permit in the United States.

To correct and refute negative or unfavorable information about Spain is another aspect of the job of the Counselor of Information and his department.

The American press is not generally favorable toward Spain,

and is often inaccurate about its facts. It commits sins of both commission and omission; in most cases, of omission.

Although they do so to a diminishing degree, the U.S. press, radio, and television tend to stress and circulate all Spanish news having a negative character. They play up strikes, upheavals, accidents, catastrophes, and student demonstrations, yet remain silent about or give little attention to news of a positive constructive nature, such as liberalization, economic progress, social advances, the contribution of Spain to the bloc of Western defense, freedom of the press and religion, and so on.

A typical example of this treatment is their reaction to Spain and Great Britain's dispute about Gibraltar.

The policy of the United States toward matters of colonialism is clear and fair, except in regard to Europe. For on the old continent, which through the efforts of Spain Christianized and civilized the New World, there continues to exist, quite outrageously and shamelessly, a colony on Spanish territory: Gibraltar. The public knows that Spain and the United States are close allies. They know that Spain permitted the installation of military bases, jointly used by her and the United States—one of the most important being the Polaris submarine base in Rota, Cádiz, just a few miles from the British military base of Gibraltar. These bases, established through bilateral agreements between the two nations, expose Spain to well-known risks and dangers. In this connection you may recall the painful atomic experience of Palomares, in order to appreciate the situation.

Because of the Gibraltar encroachment, Spain not only incurs risks from which it receives no benefit whatever, but is exposed to constant violations involving the integrity of her national territory —a situation that hurts all Spaniards regardless of their political views. The problem of Gibraltar is a political problem and should be dealt with in the United Nations. However, up to the present, with a few honorable and outstanding exceptions, U.S. news media favor the British viewpoint on Gibraltar, with no basis for this except a vast ignorance, lack of awareness of the problem, and an ancestral fear of annoying the British.

Man's memory is short indeed. It appears to be forgotten that it was Spain that helped the United States, in its struggle for independence, to rid itself of the British colonial yoke, and that today Spain is the most faithful and dependable ally of the United States.

As a typical example of this process of correcting the American press, I would like to cite an editorial published in the *Washington Post* on October 11, 1966, as well as a letter signed by me and graciously published by this paper on the 14th of the same month.

"SIEGE OF GIBRALTAR"

"In proposing to refer the dispute with Spain over the status of Gibraltar to the World Court, Britain shows full confidence in her case. Spain's renunciation of the Mediterranean rock fortress in the 1713 Treaty of Utrecht was quite explicit. The trouble is that even a new international ruling would not necessarily halt the economic blockade and other harassments Spain has been inflicting upon the 25,000 hapless residents of Gibraltar in order to penalize Britain.

"That an irredentist Spain should seek to end what she regards as a foreign anachronism at the tip of the Iberian Peninsula is understandable—though the charge of British colonialism that has produced some doctrinaire reactions in the United Nations is altogether specious. Spain has some colonial enclaves of her own—for example, the city-states of Ceuta and Melilla in Morocco—that would bear far less scrutiny than autonomous Gibraltar. In any event, at a time when so much emphasis is placed upon self-determination, the wish of the people concerned ought to be determining—and almost to a man the people of Gibraltar wish to remain British. Spain's tactics of economic squeeze could not have been more calculated to alienate them.

"Perhaps some day, when there is a different governmental attitude in Madrid, the people of Gibraltar may want to expand the natural economic and cultural links with Spain into ties of sovereignty. But an essential principle is at stake, in that whatever may be done ought to be with the consent of the governed. Not only is it important that Britain continue to respect this principle. It also is important that the United States not allow its defense interests and concern for friendly relations with Spain lead it into seeming to sanction a violation of the principle."

The following reply signed by me appeared in the "Letters to the Editor" section of the *Washington Post* of October 14, 1966:

"THE GIBRALTAR CASE"

"Readers of your newspaper do not really deserve such poor treatment of news as your editorial of Oct. 11 gives them on the Spain-Britain dispute over Gibraltar.

"It is true that according to the 1713 Treaty of Utrecht, Spain ceded the Rock-fortress of Gibraltar to Britain. But is also quite true that the same Treaty explicitly states that 'the above named property be yielded to Great Britain without any territorial jurisdiction, and without any open communication by land with the country round about.' This explains, beyond all possible doubt, the Spanish move downgrading the Spanish Customs Office at La Línea de la Concepción to a 'third class post' subject to the customs office in Algeciras and not equipped to clear movements of merchandise or automobiles, thereby halting all land trade and vehicular traffic between the Rock and the rest of Spain.

"If your editorialist fears for the future of the present inhabitants of Gibraltar—of Moroccan, Maltese, Portuguese, Hindu, Jewish, and British descent—he should ask the British Government why it attacked Spanish sovereignty on the 12th of July, stating in a formal and official way that Britain is sovereign over the isthmus contiguous to the Rock—and belonging to Spain—while at the same time it preaches protection to the population of Gibraltar.

"The Spanish reaction has been logical and mandatory.

"In this issue Spain is acting according to the United Nations General Assembly's resolution in which the procedures for the decolonization of Gibraltar were clearly established.

"If Britain 'shows full confidence in her case' proposing to refer the dispute to the International Court of Justice at The Hague, she also shows that she fears the overwhelming consensus of the United Nations which has strongly pointed out the existence of this last anachronistic colonial situation in Europe. British delaying tactics such as submitting the issue to the International Court, or alleging that the Spanish regime is not good enough for the present inhabitants of the Rock are childishly out of place considering the validity of the Spanish claim and the consensus of the United Nations. Not even the most naive could belive that if the Spanish regime were any different, England would in turn change her attitude.

"It is amazing to read in your editorial your admonition to the United States Government, warning it not to seemingly sanction the Spanish position. Spain and the United States are strongly allied. There exist important defense and military agreements that are to be renegotiated in 1968. So far Spain has proved that she is a trustworthy ally, but this does not mean that Spain can be taken for granted."

Spain, like the United States and other nations, is faced with problems it is now engaged in solving. Most important among such matters is the process of liberalization, now under way, which has begun in a concrete manner with the passage of the new Press Law that abolished censorship in 1966. This measure was followed by the new Organic Law of the State, a sort of Spanish "constitution" approved by a national referendum on December 14 of the same year. This new legislation supplements and perfects the rights statute, giving it greater stability, guarantees of order, continuity, and representation. It has numerous highly important components, among them establishment of the principle of religious freedom.

The Cabinet, with the Head of State presiding, had already approved the text of a "Bill on Religious Liberty," which was then sent to the Spanish Cortes, or Parliament, for discussion and promulgation and was passed in May 1967.

In this way Spain applies the doctrine of the Second Vatican Council expressed in the declaration on religious freedom of December 7, 1965. Now that the bill has become law, the former regime of religious tolerance is being replaced by one of freedom of worship, thus giving concrete form to what was outlined in the

Organic Law that was endorsed by the Spanish people at the recent referendum and that charged the State with "the protection of religious liberty" in terms also approved by the Holy See.

We in the information branch have had many busy hours providing information on Spain's action or religious freedom to United States media, which had little clear understanding of the situation. Briefly, let me cover some of the background for you.

Although coexistence between Catholics and members of other minority faiths has antecedents in Spanish history, and mosques and synagogues have existed side by side with Christian churches, the Spainish State in practice has always maintained the principle of its Catholic confessionalism. This was the case until the coming of Pope John XXIII and the Second Vatican Council, when the Church opened a discussion about the right to religious freedom and eventually recognized that this right must be included in the juridical system of civil society.

During the years that the problem was being discussed, and on the initiative of Spain's Minister of Foreign Affairs, the first official talks between Spanish civil and religious authorities took place for the drafting of a bill on the legal status of non-Catholic minorities. These talks resulted in the appointment of a committee in June 1960 to draft a proposed bill on religious freedom. The committee, composed of several government ministers and a group of lawyers, prepared the bill, of 45 articles, which, after approval by the Spanish hierarchy and the government, was sent to the Cortes and passed, with the appropriate modifications made in the text of the Spaniard's Charter by virtue of the new Organic Law of the State.

According to this bill the Spanish Government recognizes religious freedom as a right based on the dignity of man and assures the protection necessary so that nobody may be coerced in the legitimate use of this right. The first section also deals with the limitations on the right to this freedom: respect for the Catholic religion, in conformity with the special recognition it receives in Spain; respect for other faiths; morality; peace; coexistence; the demands of public order; and opposition to all forms of coercion in order to win proselytes to any faith or to estrange them from another. The bill of course maintains Catholicism as the official religion of the Spanish State and accords it the "special recognition" specified in the Council declaration.

The law represents an advance of exceptional importance on the way to full, conscious, and responsible personal freedom. Through its provisions non-Catholic groups and persons professing no religion are covered by a legal system protecting the liberties proclaimed by the Council. It is to be hoped that the law will consolidate this change and strengthen coexistence between the principle of special recognition of the Catholic religion and the civil right to religious freedom.

Problems of an international character that face Spain today, apart from the aforementioned colony of Gibraltar, are: Spain's need to be included in the European Common Market; relations with the North Atlantic Treaty Organization (NATO); and relations with the nations of Eastern Eurpoe.

I wish it were possible, in the space of one chapter, to discuss these vital matters in the detail that is mandatory if they are to be fully understood. In brief, however, our position is this:

Spanish trade with the Common Market is of great volume. We strive for institutionalization of Spain's relations with the EEC, and we feel, as stated by Spain's Minister of Foreign Affairs, Fernando María Castiella, that without our nation, "the coordinated economic structure of the Continent will fail." Inclusion of Spain in the EEC will be of great mutual benefit. As the Minister has said, in striving for this goal we are thinking of "the Spain our children will live in."

In his important statements the Minister has defined Spain's position on NATO as not being one of objection; on the contrary, Spain feels NATO performed undeniable service in the defense of Europe against the threat of the expansionist policy of "Stalinism" during the first critical years following World War II. Yet, the Minister continued,

"Spain has never asked to join NATO, nor is interested in belonging to it in its present form.

"Our peaceful attitude leads us to believe that the ideal course of action is to strive for a harmony among nations that will make this type of organization superfluous in the near future. But while the reality of the moment obliges us to consider coordinated defense, it must be recognized that any organization is incomplete if it ignores the existence of nations located in vital areas, nations which always feel uneasy knowing that military policy is made without their knowledge. Nobody should find it strange that they refuse to assume the risks and obligations of a military system to which they do not belong.

"It was inevitable that this reasonable Spanish policy should clash over Gibraltar, where as is well known, a member of NATO, located there because of a colonial past now condemned by all nations, offered its allies the use of this base located in Spanish territory. Let us hope that the solution of the Gibraltar problem —for which Spain has offered friendly and constructive formulas —makes it possible to overcome this source of friction and makes of Spain, if not a member of the alliance, at least a nation which has no reason to object to it."

In regard to the attitude of Spain toward Eastern European nations, the Minister concluded:

"Our anti-communism is a shield which protects us from Communist designs to use subversion as an international political weapon and to interfere in the internal affairs of other nations. But this policy does not go beyond that. Spaniards, being aware of the changes that occur in the relations among nations, will not remain indifferent to any effort toward coexistence, providing it is sincere."

Were it possible to put Spain's international activities and policies into adequate geographic, economic, and historic context, the desire for clarity and accuracy would tempt me strongly to examine a variety of such important topics as Spain's presence and policy in the United Nations or in the numerous international bodies of all kinds to which she belongs, or to speak of Spanish anticolonialism and her support of the colored peoples and the underdeveloped countries.

Instead, I shall restrict myself to a brief overview of our foreign policy and the contemporary relations engendered by it with nations of Western Europe, the Hispano-American countries, the Arab peoples, and the United States.

With Portugal, as in the Treaty of March 17, 1939, the initiation of the Iberian Pact, our relations have been fraternal and our policies parallel in all problems concerning us both. It is not, then, merely a goodwill policy; rather, what has been created and encouraged between our two countries is a cordial interchange, which has at all times yielded the best results.

With the rest of the countries of Europe Spain maintains friendly relations, although their degree of warmth varies from time to time in accordance with partisan interests of each nation's domestic policy. It will be remembered that, despite Spain's neutrality in World War II, she suffered an unprecedented international ostracism beginning in 1945; and attacks on her continued until 1951. The harsh aftermath of the blockade adversely affected Spain's economy, but her economy and international relations became continuously smoother in the succeeding years.

With France Spain's relations were not very good until 1955. By 1957, when Spain's economy had begun to recuperate from the effects of the blockade and the nation began its definite period of contemporary achievements, relations with France simultaneously improved noticeably. Since that time Hispano-French cooperation has been improving daily, up to the present moment of full and cordial mutual understanding.

With Great Britain the course of events has been similar, and the improvement in relations runs almost parallel. Nevertheless, between the two countries lies the shadow of Gibraltar, a grave affair that Spaniards regard as harmful and that our diplomacy is attempting to solve bilaterally, although it naturally does not renounce the use of the great forum provided by the United Nations.

Germany is an old friend of Spain. We were together in the Empire under Charles V, united on many occasions except during the years when the policy of equilibrium in Europe prevailed. Spain and Germany could not forget that France lay between them, for which reason their interests to some extent were in agreement. During our war Germany was one of the few that were on our side, and now Germany has been one of the first to help us economically and politically. Between our two peoples there are no problems pending, and Spain is grieved over the unjust division of a country that Europe and the world need to see united. The frequent ministerial visits between the two countries and the traditional friendship and admiration that has always existed between the two peoples are signs of an understanding that I regard as appropriate and fruitful.

In relation to the Europeanist movement, Spain has repeatedly proclaimed her European adherence, as well as her beliefs in the need for closer union and interpenetration among the peoples of the continent. Hence Spain is a full *de jure* member of the OECD and has applied for association with the European Common Market.

Outside of Europe Spanish external policy has the three major lines that I should like to summarize briefly.

1. Hispano-American Countries. Our relationship with these is intimate, cordial, and familiar. Spain feels herself to be part of the great community of peoples she helped to create, which today speak her language, pray to the same God, maintain the same culture, and are a living image of her traditions and moral values.

Everything that happens in that community interests and affects us too; all that occurs there has an almost immediate repercussion in my own land. Accordingly Spain, which believes in the future of Hispano-America, maintains a special relationship with each one of those countries and is resolved to show herself independent and free in maintaining the situation that is conferred on us by history, sentiment, and interests, and the conviction of belonging to a great family of peoples who have a right to follow their own destiny.

It may be said that Spain's Hispano-American policy can be summarized in three points: fidelity to a historic enterprise, acceptance of the changing realities of America, and support for what is permanent as against the opportunism of any temporary situation; but avoidance of all political inaction that may seek to impose political situations that are today quite outdated.

2. The Arab peoples in general. With regard to these nations Spain is also in a very special situation, though not to the same degree as with Hispano-America. Eight centuries of common life and struggle in the Peninsula, innumerable bonds of culture, art, language, sociology, and even blood between them and us, and a permanent neighborhood giving rise to all sorts of relations, are sufficient reasons for affirming that Spain is the European nation best prepared to understand and to be understood by the Arab world.

During the years of our isolation the Arabs, together with the Hispano-Americans, were our only sure friends, and it is right that they should continue to be so. With the exception of Algeria, all those countries' Heads of State have paid a cordial visit to Madrid. With all of them we have treaties of friendship, cultural affairs, technical matters, or aid; all of them have been visited by our ministers and statesmen; and in all of them Spain enjoys prestige and genuine friendship. In times of crisis between themselves or against third parties Spain has always been able to assist without intervening or participating. Our policy is based on mutual respect, cordiality of understanding, and support for the future.

With Morocco our intimacy is even closer for many historical and geographical reasons that go back to the dim past. More recently Morocco was under official Spanish protection since 1880; a series of treaties and negotiations in succeeding years culminated in the 1912 Treaty that recognized the Spanish protectorate over the north zone of the kingdom of Morocco. In 1957 a formal agreement was made for Spain to end her protectorate and to give administrative, technical, and other assistance to Morocco. As an indication of good friendship, Spain withdrew her forces from the former Protectorate before the year appointed by the 1957 agreement, and the application of all agreements for aid and cooperation came into force without the least difficulty.

Nevertheless, still standing between the two countries are certain complex though not grave problems, and diplomacy is being applied earnestly and vigorously to these matters. The path of negotiation has been chosen, and accordingly it is possible to discuss matters in an atmosphere of perfect friendship, which was even accentuated, if possible, by a meeting of the two Heads of State at Barajas on July 6, 1963. Mutual comprehension and generosity will shortly bear their fruit.

3. *Relations with the United States.* This is the third essential factor in our external policy. I will pass over the support given by

Spain to that nation in its struggle for independence, and our substantial contribution to the origin of many of the states themselves. Here I would confine myself to the present situation, tracing some of its highlights and starting with the 1953 Defensive Agreements signed by Spain and the United States.

These agreements were in reality three main documents relating to aid for mutual defense, economic aid, and defense. Their general objectives rested on the idea of self-defense in the face of the communist threat, the maintenance of peace and international security, and cooperation with other countries that sought the same objectives. The agreements came to mean Spain's entry into the great Western defense organization, the renunciation of a neutrality that had been traditional to Spain since the beginning of the nineteenth century, and the resumption of an attentive friendship interrupted for years.

The essence of the contractual obligation derived from the agreements as far as the United States is concerned, consisted in "Support for the Spanish defense effort," by supplying Spain with military, technical, and economic aid that would allow her to carry out that effort; and as regards Spain, in authorizing the United States Government to develop, maintain, and use for military purposes jointly with the Spanish Government, a series of zones and installations in Spanish territory, which remained under the flag and jurisdiction of Spain.

During the force of these agreements, relations between Spain and the United States became closer and closer. Many visits were exchanged between the U.S. Secretary of State and the Spanish Minister of Foreign Affairs. On December 21, 1959, President Eisenhower paid a memorable visit to Madrid to meet with our Head of State, and in 1961 the Secretary of State of the new Democratic administration, Dean Rusk, also visited our Head of State and Minister of Foreign Affairs in Madrid.

All these visits and interviews show the cordiality of the relations between the two countries, and at the same time how well the 1953 agreements had been working. In 1963 the Defense Agreement was renewed for five years, and it was affirmed that this must necessarily form part of the security arrangements for the Atlantic and Mediterranean zones. A new feature was a mutual guarantee of the territorial security and integrity of Spain and the United States, and mutual protection, in the sense that a threat to either country or their joint installations would affect both, and each would take such action as it considered suitable within the framework of its constitutional procedure. This declaration, which was described by the world press as an alliance, was completed by the establishment of a Joint Consultative Committee to discuss all defensive, political, and economic problems of common interest. The respective Foreign Ministers are entitled to preside at meetings of this committee.

The tragic death of President Kennedy filled the Spaniards with grief, and the Spanish Government was represented at his funeral in Washington by its Vice-President, Captain-General D. Agustín Muñoz Grandes.

Following the panoramic line of a cordial and loyal friendship, Spain, on January 29, 1964, signed an agreement for the construction and operation of a space-vehicle tracking station that is now located northwest of Madrid. This followed an earlier agreement, in 1960, for the establishment of a similar tracking station in the Canaries, which has played a vital role in the Apollo program.

To know and to understand modern Spain you must know far more about its background and its many interests than one chapter can possibly provide you. Making this additional information available in the United States is part of the continuing work of the Information Counselor. For me, and I know for my counterparts from many other governments, it is highly gratifying work, done with the realization that each item of new knowledge helps build the bridge to better understanding.

7

Instant Labels: Instant Trouble

AQIL AHMAD
PRESS ATTACHÉ
EMBASSY OF INDIA

A QIL AHMAD has been Press Attaché and head of the Indian Information Services in Washington since 1964. Born in 1930, Mr. Ahmad was graduated from the University of Allahabad in 1950 with degrees in history and economics. He took a law degree in 1953 and a master's degree in literature in 1956 from the same university.

While still in college, he edited the university magazine and won an award for an article on nationalism versus internationalism. From 1950 to 1954 he practiced law and contributed articles to English-language newspapers and magazines in India on social, political, and literary subjects. In 1954 he joined the editorial staff of one of the leading English-language dailies in India, the *Amrita Bazar Patrika*.

He entered government service in 1956 and was assigned by the Ministry of External Affairs to his first post, the Embassy of India in Cairo. Following Cairo, he served with the embassies in Khartoum (Sudan) and Jeddah (Saudi Arabia) before coming to Washington.

Mr. Ahmad is the author of *Law of Equity* (1956) and *Mohammedan Law* (1954). In 1966 both books went into fourth editions. A collection of Mr. Ahmad's Urdu poetry is also in print. Since joining the government in 1956 he has written several books and feature articles for the Indian Ministry of External Affairs and has edited embassy journals and news releases.

He lives in Washington with his wife and son.

WHEN I was asked to write this chapter I was reminded of a simple line from Indian poetry that says: "The bird-catcher laid the trap and himself fell into it." It is the profession of a public relations man to talk about others; he seldom talks about himself. I had been discussing the information problems of embassies in Washington with Professor John Lee and Dr. Ray E. Hiebert of the Washington Journalism Center. From these discussions, they tell me, came the idea for this book. Obviously, with disastrous results, I fell into my own trap. So, here I am to make confessions.

The feeling of reluctance in the public relations man to talk about himself stems from many factors, one of which, I believe, is that historically he does not find himself in very good company. We are told that the forerunners of public relations men were the priests in the primitive tribal societies and the poets in Greece, who, according to Plato, were "hired by the State to serve its welfare." The wandering minstrels of dark ages are also supposed to be forerunners of modern public relations men. The more charitable current definition describes them as "space grabbers."

A few years back some press attachés met to form an association and, very naturally, one of them suggested that the news of the meeting should receive coverage in the news media. When skeptics raised doubts, a young and more enthusiastic press attaché countered by saying, "If we cannot arrange coverage for our meeting then we are not worth our name." Next morning, we searched in vain for the news. This very clearly shows that we are not space grabbers and, I hope, explains our reluctance to talk about ourselves.

A very pertinent question can be asked as to what really is the objective of an information setup of an embassy. Well-known American public relations consultant Edward Burneys, talking once about "gaining goodwill for India," posed the question whether his role was "to give advice on policies" or "to give words to explain the policies." He concluded in favor of the latter. I feel the real role should be a combination of both.

In view of the fact that a press attaché or a public relations officer falls within the category of diplomats, we may turn to the definition of diplomats. The job of a diplomat, one definition says, is "to lie abroad." For very obvious reasons, it is difficult for me to accept this definition, either.

In the absence of a satisfactory definition I have to fall back on my own definition; that the job of an information setup is to disseminate suitable and timely information about a country and to be aware of the trends of public opinion in the country of his assignment, the three operative words being "dissemination," "suitable," and "timely."

Often it is said that the information work on behalf of a country should be categorized as advertising and that the office handling that work should not be very different from an advertising agency. This is only partly true because there is a very fundamental difference between the information office and an advertising agency. The job of an advertising agency is to sell a product, whereas the job of an information office is to sell an image. Inasmuch as a product is tangible (its returns are measured in sale proceeds and it can be modified, altered, or changed according to the market), it is very different from an image. Because the image is intangible, its projection presents many difficulties; because the image of a country, unlike a product, is composed of totality of social, political, and various other aspects of life of millions of human beings, its projection suffers from many handicaps and limitations. When one public relations consultant advised change in the policy of a country to obtain better results, the country changed the consultant instead. An advertiser would not have done so.

Information office work also differs from the work of other news media like newspaper, radio, and television, and so on. The basic difference lies in their respective approaches. For a news medium, all that is good, bad, or indifferent makes news so long as it is new and fresh. This is not so for an information office.

Because the basic objective of an information office is to project a balanced image of its country, the first duty of the office is to obtain news and information that may help in creating a favorable image. Perhaps for historical reasons the impression has been created that whatever information or material comes out of an embassy is a pack of lies or, at best, half truth. I can speak with confidence about the approach of my own office: although we do exercise discretion in selection of material, we take proper care that only accurate information is publicized.

If you permit me to digress a bit, it is not possible for us to give incorrect facts for the simple reason that India is a democracy with completely free press. Facts given by us can always be checked and verified with the facts as they appear in the press. In this very vital aspect, I think, the situation in the United States and in India is the same. Delhi has a large number of foreign press correspondents. Major newspapers of the United States and some television networks have their bureaus in Delhi. Similarly, all the major news agencies have offices in Delhi. For this reason it is not possible for the Indian Information Office to say things that cannot be substantiated. In fact, there is a story that a foreign correspondent in Delhi filed some of his most devastatingly critical stories, from our point of view, for two weeks while he was confined to bed by illness. The six national dailies of India provided the ammunition.

However, what is possible for an information setup is to highlight such facts as contribute to building a favorable image. Therefore the role of a publicity agency or an information office is a very limited one. To illustrate the point, in 1966 we published a book under the title *India: World's Largest Democracy*. Every word in this title reflects the true nature of India's political and social system. India has a parliamentary democracy. India has held three general elections based on adult franchise. The elections have been accepted as free and fair. India has complete freedom of speech and expression of views. India has an independent judiciary and free and impartial Public Service Commissions, and so on. It is the job of an information setup to make these facts known adequately in the United States, which is the second largest democracy in the world.

After suitable material has been created, the question of dissemination arises and it is at this point that an information office faces its greatest difficulty. So far as advertising agencies are concerned, the dissemination of their material is not a problem for the simple reason that the firm concerned foots the bill of the cost of space, as long as the campaign lasts. In case the advertisement utilizes other media, for example television, the cost on the basis of time is also paid by the firm. However, it is neither practicable nor advisable for a publicity office to use the channel of paid advertising for building the image of a country. This, I think, would be self-defeating. The normal and recognized vehicles for dissemination of information are news releases, distribution of books and periodicals, exhibition of films, library service, reply to individual inquiries, background briefing, special interviews, talks and speeches, and press relations.

We bring out a regular press release entitled *Indiagram*. The release gives day-to-day developments in India in the political and economic field. We who are in this business refuse to believe the unpalatable fact that the releases usually find their way to wastepaper baskets. If, luckily, our release receives a mention in the news media, our faith is strengthened. When recently a newspaper came out with a prominent headline "U.S.-India Wheat Deal Geared to Mrs. Gandhi," we put out a contradiction and were gratified to find that the news media took note of it. Earlier, a leading newspaper had taken editorial note of our press release. This happens rarely, but just often enough to keep the faith.

Our main vehicle for dissemination of information about India direct to the people is a weekly newspaper, *India News*. We try to give coverage to the important developments in various fields in one week. Inasmuch as texts of important statements, joint communiques, and resolutions are printed in the *India News*, I am told they provide useful material for reference, research, and record. For instance, the major event taking place in India while I was preparing this chapter was the Fourth General Elections for the Parliament and State Assemblies. In several issues immediately prior to the elections we tried to cover the election manifestoes of various political parties in the hope that this would provide useful information to those who would be interested in writing about the General Elections in India.

We have a moderate film library consisting of about 300 films depicting the various aspects of Indian life. We try to meet the growing number of requests for these films.

The large number of letters received daily from Americans go to show the spirit of inquiry and the desire to know more about other countries. These letters make interesting reading. The subjects range from very searching questions about the program of community development in India to a bland affirmation of opinion. I remember one such letter, which read something like this: "Dear Mr. Ambassador, I firmly believe that China did not attack India. It was India which attacked China. Yours sincerely." We begged to differ with the writer of the letter and told him the pertinent facts.

We maintain a library service at the Embassy of India that is open to all for reference purposes. It is heartening to see serious researchers sitting in the library for hours, poring over books and taking notes briskly.

In countries like the United States and India, where the information media are completely free, there is considerable demand for speakers to talk about their country and "to face the nation" in a question-answer session. An outstanding example of this medium is a luncheon address to the National Press Club, despite the very delicate controversy that occasionally arises of whether the fair sex should have representation at the function. We had our own share of this ticklish problem when our Prime Minister, Mrs. Indira Gandhi, came to this country in 1966.

The scope of background briefings is fairly restricted by two factors: (a) a background briefing can be given only at the time when some major developments are taking place at a fast pace; and (b) the person giving this briefing has to be a man of sufficient status who can speak with authority.

This brings me to the question that is fundamental to all our public information activity—the image of India as projected by the U.S. news media. It is a delicate subject, and if I were a good diplomat, I would handle it with all the subtleties; but I am a public relations man. I would much rather be honest with you.

No two nations have had so much in common, in spite of being so far apart, as India and America have today. Both have fought for freedom. Both value liberty, justice, and the dignity of man. Both are wedded to democracy and together represent more than 700 million people. Both are dedicated to the Charter of the United Nations and to peace in the world. Yet both of them sometimes are victims of misunderstanding and misgivings. In discussing India's image in the United States my attempt will be directed not only toward determining what nurtured these misgivings but also toward how we can get rid of them.

With its penchant for catchy phrases, the U.S. news media have evolved new labels to describe India. Time and again, for instance, we have explained our secularism in no uncertain terms. Over and over, the news media have labeled us as "Hindu India."

Here is a specimen story. "A Hindu holy saint of Hindu India went on fast today in Puri, a town in the eastern state of Orissa, which is venue of a religious festival attracting large crowds of Hindu pilgrims. . . ." The repeated use of the word "Hindu" in a four-line story is striking. It is like saying "A Christian priest of Christian America speaking in a Christian church." Hindus are, no doubt, in a majority in India, but there are over 55 million Muslims, 15 million Christians, 1 million Sikhs, and a sizable population of Buddhists, Zoroastrians, Jews, and others. The State has no religion and prefers none. It treats people of all faiths alike, even those who choose not to adhere to any faith. When one uses the phrase "Hindu India," he gives us the impression that he understands neither Indian culture nor Indian history. The synthesis of Indian culture is tolerance. As a result, today we have a multireligious and multilingual society. The term "Hindu India" is inconsistent with the very fundamental of our political system and our society.

Another label we do not appreciate is "Hungry India" as the term for our economic posture. It distorts the true picture of the development programs. It undermines the efforts we have made in ameliorating the lives of 500 million people.

In a recent social meeting when a not-too-friendly American friend went on hurling the phrase "Hungry India," it evoked indignant reaction from an Indian visitor. Thereupon the American friend very rightly posed the question: "Aren't people dying of hunger in India?" only to bring forth an equally caustic reply, "Aren't people dying of overeating in this country?" The moral of the story is that such labels to describe complex situations betray ignorance of facts and are based on prejudices.

Drought for two successive years did, indeed, create a famine situation in some parts of the country, but to describe us as "Hungry India" seems to be a poor delineation of our passing difficulty. The food shortage was localized in some parts of the country only and there were no deaths from hunger. Of the 17 states in India, 12 are self-sufficient in food production. In 1950 we produced about 50 million tons of food-grain. In 1964 to 1965, we had a record production of 88 million tons and imports did not exceed 7 million tons. All these facts now told, I ask you if you would caption the story as "Hungry India"?

A full-page picture story about India containing photographs of Indian slums appeared recently in an important U.S. daily newspaper and brought forth a reply that is revealing. "Your picture story on India," wrote Mr. Frank Stedman Wilson, a businessman with more than 15 years of residence in India,

"fills me with dismay. May I reinterpret India to your readers: INDIA—A land of growing prosperity, with a greater number of prosperous people than all of England, as well as some who are still very poor. A country, not of 500 million poor, but of 50 million prosperous urban citizens; another 50 million who know they are better off each passing year; a further 350 million living on the land, as their farmer ancestors did before them, most of whom are a bit better fed, thanks to their own more vigorous efforts, than they were 10 years ago; and finally, something under one-tenth of the people who are indeed in want. A country whose birth rate has declined from a high of 48 per thousand in this century to under 42. A country whose death rate has dropped even more dramatically (and for this we Americans may take a small measure of credit)—but nevertheless a nation whose increase in food supply by its own efforts is more than one-and-one-half times the increase in its population. Certainly India needs our help and will continue to do so for quite a few years to come. But let this not detract from the massive and solid achievements of the government and people of India. Above all, there is a determination on the part of India's people that the good life shall be more freely available hereafter for the children of all and not of just the few. This is Indian democracy in action and we wish it well. I hope that your roving photographer will turn his penetrating camera on all facets of Indian life, including her beauty and her pride in her growing prosperity."

India is a poor country. We have all the problems of a developing country, and more. But this is half the story. The other half, I think, is best summed up by Lester Markel in his article, "The Myths That Divide India and Us," published in the *New York Times Magazine*. I quote:

"But there are other sights that are symbols of hope . . . the model farms and the bustling factories . . . the younger generation, fighting tradition and lethargy . . . the girls in the offices, charming, sparkling and competent . . . the students eager to learn and in turn to instruct their parents . . . the deep dedication of the teachers . . . the women at the village clinic, wholly concentrated on the task of learning new methods . . . the new breed of Government officials, intent on breaking through the shackles of habit, corruption and inefficiency."

The myth that "if you are not for us, you are against us" died long ago. We still live, however, with the image of "Neutral India." It seems so paradoxical to us that a nation that, not too long ago, pursued policies avoiding foreign entanglements should condemn us for following the same course today. You chose to stay aloof from the bickerings of the colonial nations of Europe. We have chosen today to stay away from the power polarizations. Times are, of course, different, but there remains an identity in the objectives of our policies.

India is not neutral but is a nonaligned nation. We have pointed out the difference between the two terms many times, and I shall do it again: neutrality means not taking part in war; nonalignment, to us, means that we are not committed to anyone and reserve the right, as a sovereign nation, to judge each issue on its merits. It is our conviction that alignments could precipitate war. It is also our conviction that by being nonaligned we can serve the cause of world peace as we have done in Korea, the Congo, the Middle East, and in Indo-China.

How strange it is that the same two powers—the United States and the U.S.S.R.—that we were being forced to choose between yesterday are applauded today for their cooperation. And how strange even that we are still being assailed as "Neutral India."

It is saddening to note that one U.S. newspaperman had to travel all the way from here to India to discover "India's long record of violence." It is more saddening that an important newspaper found it worth publishing. The conclusion of the learned newspaperman is based on the facts that India liberated Goa, that riots do take place in India, and that India fought wars with China and Pakistan, wars that were not of her choosing. What our friend perhaps wanted was for Indians to sit back in meditation and face the bullets. It is clear from the story that the writer was laboring with a prejudiced mentality. Indians do not claim any higher moral standards than the rest of the world. However, India stands for world peace and has, I feel, a proud record of efforts in that direction. To travel thousands of miles for making an on-the-spot study only to report biased conclusions based on events that took place years ago is *not,* to my mind, correct journalism.

We thought that we had laid the ghost of Goa at rest. Obviously there are people who suffer from nostalgia.

Before her independence India had three masters occupying different parts of the country: there were the British, the French, and the Portuguese. The first two left after a long period of persuasion, but we were still saddled with the Portuguese for 15 years after independence. We used every occasion and every single channel of communication to urge them to leave. The matter finally came to a standstill and we were told that Goa in India was an integral part of Portugal.

We had said that we would not use force in Goa. We could not, however, accept Portugal's contention that Goa was an integral part of her territory. Geographically, culturally, and historically, Goa has been part of Indian territory. If we had received some response or indication from the Portuguese in regard to their future departure from Goa—not necessarily an early departure— we would have refrained from using force. During the last moments of our police action, as you may know, the United States tried to intervene. She was politely told, by the government of Portugal, that Goa was an internal matter of Portugal.

We were stunned at the American criticism of our action in

Goa. It was incomprehensible for us that the United States, which proclaimed the Monroe Doctrine to protect the independent states in the Western Hemisphere from the colonial powers of Europe, and which has since supported independence movements, would criticize us so vehemently for washing off a small spot of colonialism from our land.

In the area of labels, India recently was given brief exposure to one for which all we residents of Washington sometimes are thought to qualify: that of being dedicated drinkers. A correspondent of a leading television network flew to India for a study of drought in the state of Bihar and made much of the fact that some leaders in the state capital were drinking whisky. Regardless of the factual verification of the report, a hypothetical parallel might be that "because young American boys are dying in Vietnam, every American has stopped drinking whisky." With this biased approach, it is no wonder that he did not see anything good in India during his brief trip.

The label "Socialist India" is often used by the American news media. It is designed to give the impression of the public control of economy. Far from this, private enterprise has widest possible scope in India and is thriving very well. The news media seem to be reluctant to adopt the word that Indians use to describe their economy. We call it a policy of "mixed economy," in which the private and the public sectors have fullest scope for development. They are meant to coexist and they are coexisting. As Mrs. Indira Gandhi, Prime Minister of India, recently said: "Our socialism is one that is related to the reality of the Indian situation. It is not wedded to any dogma. What we all want is a better life, with more food, employment, and opportunities. Let us not become prisoners of words."

A letter written by Mr. Ernest Weatherall of CBS Radio, New York, makes a very revealing study of the attitude of the news media towards India. The letter was published in the *New York Times*. Mr. Weatherall says,

"As a former correspondent in New Delhi, I can honestly say it is not the fault of the newsmen assigned there that so little information about India reaches Americans back home. With the exception of *The Times* and a few other newspapers, most editors depend on wire service coverage of India. And, unfortunately, most of the dispatches never get beyond an editor's wastepaper basket. Editors have told us that there is not enough space with the Vietnam war the No. 1 foreign news story (before it was the Korean war, the cold war and so on). Editors have also told us that there is no 'spot news' in India, unless there is a riot in New Delhi or a holy man fails to walk on water. The editors' final reasoning is that their readers are 'just not interested in India.' "

Lest I may be guilty of giving a label to the American news media, I would hasten to point out that there are some very prominent exceptions to what I have said earlier. Some of the correspondents, especially those based in India, have, by and large, done objective reporting and have tried to rise above labels and catchy phrases. They often differ and criticize our programs and policies. We do not object to an honest and fair criticism, as it invariably heals more than it hurts. Objective criticism is an invaluable asset of democratic societies. But how can we be objective if we do not understand each other?

The world of communications is progressing and changing as rapidly as the world. Tomorrow's journalists, like today's, will still have the grave responsibility of reporting and interpreting not only their own society but others as well. There are no easy ways of discharging this responsibility. It is the easy way that creates images inversely related to the realities.

8

The Streamlining of John Bull

PAUL H. G. WRIGHT, C.M.G., O.B.E.
MINISTER (INFORMATION)
THE BRITISH EMBASSY

DIRECTOR-GENERAL
BRITISH INFORMATION SERVICES
NEW YORK

P AUL H. G. WRIGHT was born in 1915 and was educated at Westminster School, London, one of the oldest and most famous boys' schools in Britain. He began his working life in 1933 with a large chain-store organization, and stayed with the firm until the outbreak of World War II, when he enlisted in the army. He served with the King's Royal Rifle Corps, the famed "Greenjackets," a regiment originally raised in America to fight Indians. He rose to the rank of major, and served on Field Marshal Montgomery's staff during the Normandy landings and the subsequent campaign in Europe.

In 1948 he was appointed Director of Public Relations for the Festival of Britain and was awarded the O.B.E. (Officer, Most Excellent Order of the British Empire) for his services in this capacity. He was appointed to the United Nations Mission in 1951, then transferred to the Foreign Office in 1954. In 1956 he joined the staff of the British Embassy at the Hague. He returned in 1957 to the Foreign Office, where he was promoted to Counselor and became Head of the Information Policy Department.

Mr. Wright was created a Commander of the Most Distinguished Order of St. Michael and St. George (C.M.G.) in the Queen's Birthday Honours of 1960 and sent to Cairo as Chargé d'Affaires. In 1961 he was transferred to the United Kingdom Delegation to NATO in Paris.

He became Director-General of British Information Services, New York, in 1964, and to this appointment was added that of Minister (Information) in the British Embassy in Washington in 1965. He lives in New York with his wife, Beatrice, an American whom he married during the war.

I DID not choose the title of this article, although I think it is a good one. At least I thought it was good until I began to wonder what it actually meant—"The Streamlining of John Bull." Then I realized that I did not know who John Bull was. I wonder how many of you know who Uncle Sam is or how he originated?

I looked up John Bull; it is a fascinating story. He first appears in 1712 in a satire by John Arbuthnot about the French wars. The piece is a humorous allegory, dealing with the cessation of the wars in France. There were John Bull and Nicholas Frog (who, incidentally, represented the Dutch), Lord Strut (Philip of Spain), and Louis Baboon (the French King). The description of John Bull given in 1712 is interesting. Mr. Arbuthnot says,

"He's described as an honest, plain-dealing fellow—chloreric, bold and of a very inconstant temper, very apt to quarrel with his best friends, especially if they pretended to govern him. John's temper depended very much upon the air. His spirits rose and fell with the weatherglass. John was quick and understood his business very well, a boon companion, loving his bottle and his diversions."

We have now got to see whether he has been streamlined at all. I do not know whether streamlining means losing weight. It's an odd word to apply to a person, but it's a rather good word to apply to a nation. It *is* what is happening in Britain. We are being streamlined.

Before discussing that, however, I want to talk about something else that is, in a sense, more important. These problems cannot be discussed without taking into account the picture that each country has of the other. And in this respect, in the picture we—the British and the Americans—have of each other there have always been, and there still are, a great many myths.

I am not going to discuss the over-all view of the Americans that is now prevalent in Europe, but some of the myths in that view. We all know what they are—that Americans are all frightfully rich and materialistic; that they have no culture; that they are power-mad (whether in automobiles or armies); that they have trigger-happy generals and hatchet-faced Wall Street bankers; and that everyone smokes cigars. Now, like the reports of Mark Twain's death, this view is greatly exaggerated. Of course, we all know this, and as people travel more a lot of these myths get exploded. But some of them are still there; and they are dangerous.

When you look at the picture the other way round—the American view of Britain—it is rather more complicated because there are two sets of myths. There is the old-fashioned myth that the British are stuffy; that they all wear monocles and Bowler hats, and are all lords and ladies; that they mumble and drawl, live in the past, are usually dressed up in some fancy kind of costume, and live in drafty castles with no central heating (and certainly no plumbing); that they all have a stiff upper lip and never show any emotion; that all men smoke a pipe and read the *London Times*. Mixed in with this in the last few years there has been another set of myths—that is, that everyone is swinging and wears a miniskirt; that the place is full of gambling shops, and no one works; that British industry has not progressed since the nineteenth century; and that Britain has lost an empire.

Here, again, I think these pictures are no truer of Britain today than the picture that some have in Europe of the average American. But these images do emerge, especially through the mass media, magazines, television, and radio. I think we should try and get some of this into perspective. I do not want to pretend that everything is right with Britain, because it is not. We all know that. We are not complacent, and we are having a great dose of self-criticism ourselves. That is all to the good. The things that are not right about Britain should be recorded, and our problems aired and discussed with our friends. Britain ought to be reported, I think, warts and all, as Oliver Cromwell once said about himself.

Just because everything is not all right, however, everything is by no means all wrong. I want to correct some of these myths because I think that the fashionable view of Britain as a sort of has-been nation that is gracefully, gaily even, sinking to the status of a minipower is a dangerous cliché. It is dangerous for us because a nation's well-being depends in part on the view and the confidence in it held by its friends abroad; and it is dangerous for the United States because in spite of America's power she needs friends and strong, dependable allies, especially those like Britain, with whom the things she has in common really greatly outweigh the points of divergence and disagreement.

How do we see our position in the world today? First of all, we accept the fact that Britain cannot expect to wield the same influence today in world affairs as she did when we were the center of a far-flung empire. However, we believe that we are entitled to the credit for having dismantled that empire in a systematic and orderly way, recognizing the political and economic realities of the twentieth century. We have tried to retain for the world at large the benefits that we believe come from cooperation between a cross section of peoples of the world, of different cultures and races. Therefore we have created and are helping to maintain the conception of the commonwealth.

People criticize the commonwealth as being merely a talking shop; but a talking shop can have a very valuable use in the twentieth century. The fact that it remains as a multiracial association of free peoples is in itself an important factor. At the same time we have taken a leading part in the various defensive organizations of the world like NATO and SEATO, and, in particular, in the economic affairs of Europe—in OEEC and the European Free Trade Association. Furthermore, as everyone knows, we are now embarking on a new effort to get closer economic ties with the Common Market countries. And at the risk of overtaxing our own strength, we are making a large contribution to the defense of the free world, not only in Europe, but in the Middle East and in South East Asia.

Our basic problem at the present time, with which we are all deeply concerned, is the British economy, its strength, and its future.

The first difficulty is the change in status from an empire to a single island. It has meant losses in manpower and in material, both greatly exaggerated by our experiences in the two world wars. These factors have brought about a fundamental change in the environment of the British economy. It is very difficult to maintain growth in a modern competitive industrial society if the environment in which that economy is set is shrinking. We are a highly prosperous country; we always have been and we still are. Britain accounts for 7 percent of the productive capacity of the free world; for 9 percent of all world trade; for 14 percent of world exports of manufactured goods. Every week of the year Britain exports 280 million dollars worth of goods. These are just a few basic figures that show that our problem is not poverty or lack of prosperity; it is much more complex. For one thing, rising standards of living—and this is common to most developed countries in the free world—have led to a continually rising consumer demand, leading to economic spiral that has been very difficult for us to get out of: balance of payment difficulties, too much money being spent out of the country, not enough money for home investment, and so forth.

Another problem is the fact that our defense expenditure, which is very high in proportion to most other countries', is especially heavy in hard currency across the exchanges. In addition, we have had to try to maintain contributions to the less developed countries in terms of aid.

This has been a big adjustment for the British to face and it is only since World War II that the process has caught up with us. The momentum increased as more and more of the commonwealth countries became independent, a process that is now virtually complete. Despite all this there are certain things that we have achieved. We have changed fundamentally the structure of our visible trade balance. That means that between 1946 and 1964 our visible exports rose in volume by 150 percent, and they now pay for 95 per cent of all our imports—instead of only about two-thirds, as was the case in 1938. This is an enormous change in the pattern of the nation's economy. There has also been a major change in the geographical distribution of our overseas trade. A lot of it used to be with the commonwealth. Now a much higher proportion is with the United States. We have also maintained a reasonably steady growth in the gross national product, just under 3 percent. And we have done all this while maintaining a higher degree of full employment than any other country in the world.

Now, let me elaborate a little bit on this. People say our industries are old-fashioned and that our products are noncompetitive. You can certainly find evidence for this, as you can in any developed country. It is interesting, however, that the fastest-growing exports from Britain have been in precisely those modern manufactured products that would be expected from a vigorous industrial country: chemicals, metals, engineering products. And the fastest-growing export trade has been with the sophisticated markets of the United States and the industrialized countries of Europe. All this seems to suggest that the picture is not quite as black as it is painted.

We have also built up and maintained a first-class system of credit finance and insurance; this is a positive factor because London remains one of the banking centers of the world and we have still got the resources to back such a system.

We have also managed to keep a flow of investment overseas, about a third of which has gone to the less developed countries. At the same time we have had to maintain an outlay, on the average, of about 7 percent of our gross national product on defense at home and abroad. This is a greater proportion than any other country in the world is spending on defense in foreign currency, including the United States. This too has been a big drag on our economy, and the crises that have so often hit the headlines have not been so much crises in the British economy itself as difficulties in our balance of payments. Certainly some of our economic difficulties are due to unique factors such as the fact that we have to import around 35 to 40 percent of the food we eat and at least 50 percent, and in some cases much more, of our raw materials and semifinished materials in order to keep our industries going. This bill has got to be met every month.

It is not so much the problem of production at home; it is not the basic question of prosperity or wages—indeed, sometimes it is a question of overprosperity. Increased prosperity means increased demand, which, in Britain, leads to more imports; and unless there are more exports to pay for them we are inevitably faced with an increased deficit in our balance of payments.

Turning to another aspect of life, that of new ideas, since 1945 no less than 22 British scientists have received the Nobel Prize. These awards have represented major breakthroughs in many branches of science and technology in the immediate post-war period.

We hear a good deal about the "brain drain" from Britain and I would like now to give you some figures about that. It is not quite so spectacular as it is sometimes made out to be. For example, there has been a great deal of publicity lately in the United Kingdom and also over here about the drainage of doctors away from the United Kingdom. Our latest estimates of emigration of physicians is between 300 and 400 a year. However, in the country as a whole there are 60,000 active civilian doctors, and new doctors are qualifying at the rate of 1600 a year. Those are 1965 figures. By 1970 that figure of 1600 is expected to reach about 2800. Out of that, 300 to 400 a year is not a very serious loss. Some of these emigrants, who go to the United States and a number of other countries, do not stay permanently. They may stay for perhaps six or seven years and then return home—and this of course is greatly to our gain. They come back with new ideas, new experiences, new techniques, and, above all, new friends.

Another interesting aspect of the "brain drain" is that the emigration of experts in all the fields of management, administrative and technical, is nearly balanced by the inflow of similar technicians and qualified managers from Western Europe and the commonwealth. The figures are something like 47,000 leaving to 42,000 entering.

The last point I would like to make is more philosophical. I believe that one of the problems in both our countries is that we all expect to see results much too quickly. It seems clear, however, that acutely difficult problems such as Vietnam and Rhodesia are not likely to be resolved quickly. So it is with a nation's development. We have got used to quick news, quick images on the television, instant culture of all kinds, and we tend to forget that countries, large units, large communities take a very long time to evolve.

In Britain we are going through a kind of evolutionary process. One of the reasons the British image is so confused in the United

States is because it is in a sense also confused at home. We are in a great state of flux. This is especially true of young people in Britain. They are constantly—and I am thankful for it—trying to find new ways of expressing themselves. British industry is undertaking a serious managerial revolution. Our educational system is changing far more rapidly than anybody realizes, with the creation of many new universities. The arts today are available to the community in a far more general way than they were when I was a boy 25 years ago. More important, there are big changes in the social structure of the country. One of the myths about the British that was at least half true is that we were very much a class society. I believe that the old barriers between the classes are being broken down rapidly, and the whole mass of the people is taking a much more positive and active part in the nation's life.

While all this is going on it is difficult to see a pattern or to picture what the country is going to look or feel like in another 20 years. I think that we must watch and be patient and realize that a great many things are starting now, the fruits of which we may not see for a long time.

Some developments that we are beginning to see now started 10 or 15 years ago. The Germans, as you know, very obligingly knocked down some of our worst housing during the war, in Coventry and various other places. It takes a long time to build a city and even longer to plan it, and because we were short of basic raw materials and money after the war it has taken us even longer to rebuild these cities. But they are now springing up, and they contain a great many new ideas, both in terms of physical development of the city and of the spiritual environment in which its people live. All this was hard to see 10 or 15 years ago. Similarly, especially perhaps in the industrial sphere, a lot of seeds are now being planted, the results of which we may not see for a long time.

So the streamlining of John Bull is a process that is going on continually. I don't think the old boy has lost his fat paunch yet, nor do I think that he has developed entirely the right or the new muscles that are required to deal with the present era. But the process is happening, and happening perhaps much faster than we realize.

9

The Challenge of South Africa

WILHELMUS GERHARDUS MEYER
INFORMATION COUNSELOR
EMBASSY OF SOUTH AFRICA

WILHELMUS GERHARDUS MEYER was born in Cape Province, South Africa, in 1922. He was educated at the University of Stellenbosch, with majors in history and geography.

After a brief journalism career, during which he was a reporter for *Die Burger* in Cape Town and sports editor for *Die Oosterlig* in Port Elizabeth, he joined the government in 1951 as an Information Officer. He served first in Pretoria, then went to the South African Embassy in Brussels as Press Attaché. In 1959 he was Press Attaché to the South African Accredited Diplomatic Mission in Salisbury (at that time the capital of the Federation of Northern and Southern Rhodesia and Nyasaland).

He came to Washington early in 1967 as Information Counselor to the South African Embassy, bringing his wife and two children.

I N our world of today, imbued with a driving sense of internationalism, governed increasingly by the power of public opinion, and, through modern communications, compacted to little more than a small island, it has become a most exacting task to keep the image of a country acceptable to all.

By the same token it is also of paramount importance for a country to have its statements and actions understood by this world of which it is a part.

Very little that happens on the national front is without international significance, interest, or bearing. A country today is not only part of the world; the world has become its neighbor.

Gone are the days when a domestic problem could be solved within the privacy of the family. Neither can a statesman in our present open society with impunity make one statement for his home public and another for the international audience. Both the family argument and the statesman's deliberations are news —and news today is both international and instantaneous. Via television and its communication satellites a viewer becomes host in his own living room to a statesman in Paris being interviewed simultaneously by journalists shooting questions at him from studios in London and Washington—and to think that only in 1942 the late Joseph Stalin said that if he could control the motion picture industry of America, he would convert the entire world to communism!

It is a matter for conjecture, however, whether our fast communications or the increasing power of public opinion wields the most influence. No government under any system today can afford, within the limits of its responsibilities and principles, the luxury of knowlingly acting in a manner contrary to the wishes of its peoples. Public opinion has become a force to be reckoned with, both nationally and internationally. It follows also that for good government in both these spheres, the nurturing of a *responsible* public opinion has become something of a prerequisite.

It was not surprising, therefore, to hear the Vice-President of the United States, on his return from a trip to Europe recently, expressing both surprise and concern at the fact that some actions of his country were so grossly misunderstood in Europe.

It is only further proof that however commendable the ideal of international brotherhood, a critical public opinion, and effective communication media may be as symbols of progress, they present individually and collectively great challenges to any country and its information service.

What problems, for example, do they present to South Africa?

By an interplay of the forces mentioned above—forces that can be influenced to a limited degree but never fully controlled—South Africa has gained an international image that does not reflect the facts.

The egalitarian, for example, has fathered the myth that South Africa is a country peopled by some 17 million individuals of whom approximately 3.5 million *happen* to be white settlers and the rest blacks, native to the country. They maintain also that except for this chance difference in pigmentation the country has a unitary population, equally sharing a common nationhood.

It is understandable why this presentation is accepted widely and without reserve by people in Western countries. They are accustomed to a population that is predominantly white and in which any newcomer settling there is absorbed into the community, irrespective of pigmentation of skin.

It follows, therefore, that in judging the South African situation on the information given them they automatically equate the position with that in their own country. The suggested solution to any problems South Africa may be experiencing in this respect is naturally the one tried, tested, and perfected by their governments.

Yet only a cursory glance at the history of South Africa confounds both this convenient premise and suggested simple solution. At no point in time was South Africa blessed with a unitary population. The account of how a white population movement from Europe and black migration from the north of Africa converged upon the virtually uninhabited southern part of Africa and there established themselves not as one nation but as a number of distinctly different nations has been recorded by historians.

The white migrants from Europe, by force of circumstances during the last 300 years, developed their own nationalism and established a nation as inseparable from Africa as any other black nation on the whole of that vast continent.

Time proved that the differences existing between the African nations that emigrated to South Africa were so marked and fundamental that there exist to this day no less than seven distinct African nations in South Africa.

This distinction between nations in South Africa is not the brainchild of a political party or government to conform to a certain partisan policy. It was, among others, conceded and written into history by a constitutional act of the British Government in 1910.

By the South Africa Act of 1909 they established a Union of South Africa comprising most of White British South Africa and most of Black British South Africa. The same act, however, also excluded from this union three of the conglomeration of African peoples in British South Africa—the Basuto, the Swazi, and the Bechuana. Borders were defined to the territories of these three peoples, two of which—Botswana and Lesotho—gained their independence in 1966. Swaziland, the third of these protectorates, has been promised independence within the next three years.

I have dealt at some length with these aspects mainly because they encompass the basis on which both the case for and the case against South Africa are argued.

In considering any matter pertaining to South Africa the proponents of universalism—and all their cotravelers who have joined the bandwagon by conviction or for their own ulterior motives—will, undaunted by history or present events, reach an evaluation only after testing it against their theory of race relations. Whether their conclusions are practical or realistic is of no concern to them. They are theorists; they have researched, investigated, analyzed, compared, weighed the facts as they see and interpret them, and then duly submitted their considered opinions, conclusions, solutions, or proposed plans for remedial action for the world to endorse.

That they are a dedicated group can be gleaned from the enthusiasm with which they set about the task of giving international prominence to their views and proposed actions. Thanks to their efforts, protests against South Africa have been formulated over the past 18 years in well over 100 resolutions at the United Nations, and South Africa's right to act as guardian in South West Africa was disputed in a drawn-out case in the International Court in the Hague.

At every possible occasion South Africa has been presented to the world as a despicable monster, governed as a police state by racists practicing a policy of oppression contrary to all accepted moral standards and religious concepts; no less than a threat to world peace.

Although believing ears for these presentations have been and are still being found, facts and events to the contrary are being heeded and even studied with increasing curiosity. Here I would like to call to mind a remark once made by your Secretary of State Dean Rusk, which to me is also very appropriate in our present subject. He said: "The thinking process that man uses in cases where it is necessary only to reach a conclusion is far different from the thinking processes that must result in a decision for action."

Applied to South Africa one could state without the slightest fear of contradiction that because it was the first and only nation forced to produce a solution to a multinational problem unique in the history of mankind, it also has the longest history of thinking about the problem and a possible solution thereof.

South Africa could not afford the luxury of theorizing and submitting possible solutions conforming to popular world opinion. It lived with the problem that it had to solve in the interest and to the satisfaction of a heterogeneous population: the task of successfully guiding the growth of many nations in a geographic area as yet undemarcated by national boundaries.

The real South Africa built in the process of time and differing so absolutely from its present international image is indeed a monument to this selfless dedication. America is justly proud of the fact that with only about 6 percent of the world's population, she produces 33 percent of the world's goods.

South Africa can boast a comparable record:

With barely 6 percent of the population of the African continent, and only 4 percent of its land area, it produces some 40 percent of its entire industrial output and generates 20 percent of the continent's total geographic income.

South Africa's industrial complex is unparalleled in Africa. Her mineral production represents 43 percent of the whole of Africa. She also generates twice as much electricity and produces 10 times as much steel as the rest of Africa conbined.

South Africa's mineral wealth is practically limitless. More than 50 minerals are mined, leading the world in the production of gold, gem diamonds, platinum, and antimony.

South Africa trades with the world; in 1966 about 30 percent of America's total exports to Africa went to South Africa.

Foreign investment in South Africa is in excess of 5.6 billion dollars, with America's share estimated at between 489 and 650 million dollars.

Finally, according to the United Nations, South Africa is the only developed country on the continent of Africa and one of the 26 developed areas in the world.

To any objective analyst, these figures tell the story not only of a rich and prosperous country with a buoyant economy and a lucrative trade, but also of a thriving population. They are the two interdependents in the growth of a country.

In South Africa the development of its human material more than kept pace with its national growth. Despite many difficulties and challenging problems, the population, both black and white, grew in numbers, improved its know-how, its education, and, with better opportunities of employment, its general standard of living. A vigorous education program was launched to eliminate illiteracy throughout the country, and it is hoped that this ideal will be reached within this generation.

There exists in South Africa a medicare program for its black people second to none anywhere in the world. One of the hospitals in this scheme is Baragwanath, which is not only the biggest hospital on the continent of Africa, but one of the biggest in the

Southern Hemisphere. Here no less than 2000 inpatients and a similar number of outpatients are treated on an average each day. These patients pay the negligible charge of 70 cents, irrespective of the type of medical or surgical treatment they get or whether they are hospitalized or not. The hospital also serves as a training center for Bantu nurses.

The political development of the country was realistic and in keeping with the requirements of the rather unique circumstances. Having jealously guarded their own customs and traditions for many generations—and at times under the most trying circumstances—the blacks native to a specific part of South Africa would hardly have taken lightly to future schemes for constitutional developments that disregarded these fundamentals.

Seven distinct Bantu groups, each feeling strongly about its individuality as a separate entity, became the basis for the future development of harmonious race relations in South Africa. The ultimate goal is the creation of equal black states in which each of these nations will be in a position to manage its own affairs and be the equal in every respect to the whites in the country. These separate states for blacks and whites will, however, be bound together in a commonwealth or common market based on political independence and economic interdependence.

An indication of how this will work is to be found in the present healthy relationship between South Africa and Lesotho, a British African Protectorate that gained its independence in October 1966. An enclave in South Africa, Lesotho is, among others, economically very dependent on that country—in very much the same manner as South Africa's own developing Bantu nations will be when they reach full independence.

South Africa has on numerous occasions explained her policy to the world. She has indicated that she considers herself to be an integral part of Africa, that she has no other intention but to live in peace and harmony with other African states, and that her experience and know-how are at the disposal of any African state desiring accepted international relations with her.

The race explosion in the South African crucible, predicted with so much confidence and conviction by her adversaries that at least a section of world opinion sees the country as a threat to world peace, has to date not yet materialized.

Instead the development has been so peaceful, obviously successful, and to the mutual advantage of the population as a whole, whether black, white, or colored, that South Africa has for a score or more years now been burdened with the problem of illegal black immigration from adjoining territories. It is estimated that they number more than 800,000 at the present moment.

Although South Africa has also not been spared any of the trials and tribulations common to a multiracial community, serious race disturbances have been so rare that the *Washington Post* in the spring of 1967 had to use a photograph taken seven years ago to illustrate that unrest of this nature does, in fact, occur.

The last decade in the rest of Africa has not been nearly so calm as in South Africa. Of its 48 states, 35 had gained independence during this time. To them it was a period of turmoil, strife, and adaptation to new circumstances, which often took the form of emotional outbursts on both the national and international front.

With so many trying to curry favor with the black men in Africa, mainly for their international support and vote at the United Nations, it was to be expected that South Africa would be singled out as a target for their wrath. These African states resolved to have no truck with this country of oppression, that they would do all in their power to have it isolated internationally in every possible sphere, and that they would discontinue all relations with it until such time that it changed its reprehensible race policies.

However, the possibility of a white South Africa living together with blacks on a nation-to-nation basis now seems to be gaining momentum.

In January 1967 the Prime Minister of the independent African state of Lesotho conferred in Cape Town with the Prime Minister of South Africa.

Three months later South Africa was host to three African ministers from the independent African state of Malawi. On this goodwill visit they met with the Prime Minister, conferred with members of his cabinet, and concluded a trade agreement with the Republic.

The suggestion by a leading African statesman that South Africa be readmitted as a participating member to the Economic Commission on Africa, from which it was ousted some years ago, was reported in American papers during April 1967.

These, then, are some of the more pertinent factors that come to one's attention when scrutinizing the South African scene or reading about the country in newspapers, publications, magazines, or books. Whatever set of factors or combination of fact and/or fiction of this intriguing country is presented to the uninformed outsider, chances are that he will be confused.

To an information service this is most important, particularly if seen in conjunction with the fact that it is generally the sensational, the unusual, that claim the headlines in the world press of today.

In South Africa's case, world rejection of her policies is a further determining factor in the presentation of news from that country. It is evidenced in the accentuation of the negative and an abbreviation or total omission of the positive in the news from that source.

How, then, do we as an information service set about our task of presenting our country to the world? Although hailing from Africa, even *we* have no magic formula; it has to be done by way of the spoken and written word, by sound, by image, by personal contact, and through the kind offices of friends throughout the world who believe as emphatically as the best South African in the right of all citizens of that country to a peaceful place under the African sun.

One fundamental principle, however, guides our whole campaign: the principle of truth. South Africa has staked its whole future on the belief that truth will prevail, that deeds speak louder than words. In that conviction our case is presented to the world. Many are the times that it seems a slow and unrewarding task. Never, however, can our efforts be relaxed. It is in our own interest, in the interest of the continent of which we are a part, and the interest of the Western society of nations of which we are a member, that we continue to state our case to the world in the conviction that understanding breeds friendship, and friendship, love, and love, peace.

10

Promoting Czechoslovakia in the United States

MILOSLAV CHROBOK
SECOND SECRETARY (PRESS AND POLITICAL
AFFAIRS), EMBASSY OF THE CZECHOSLOVAK
SOCIALIST REPUBLIC

MILOSLAV CHROBOK was born in Czechoslovakia in 1933. He received his secondary education at the Gymnasium in Frýdek-Místek, then studied law at the Charles' University in Prague and international law and international relations at the Moscow State Institute for International Relations in Moscow.

He worked in the foreign journalists' department of the Press Section of the Ministry of Foreign Affairs in Prague from 1959 to early 1962, then took charge of the American desk in the North American Section of the Foreign Ministry.

In 1963 Mr. Chrobok was transferred to the Embassy of the Czechoslovak Socialist Republic in Washington. His diplomatic rank is Second Secretary of the embassy and he is in charge of press and political affairs.

With him in Washington are his wife, Drahomíra, and his three children. The youngest, Olga, was born in Washington.

THE original plan of this collection of discourses by government information people called for me to write a chapter on "Prague, Protocol, and the Press." The heading was listed as "tentative," but knowing too well that one of the very basic truths about everything tentative is its tendency to become permanent, I intended to leave it without necessarily trying to live up to its promises in the chapter itself. Nevertheless, after I finished my notes and found that there was almost nothing on Prague or the protocol or the press as such, I had to capitulate and invent a title that certainly doesn't sound exciting but probably corresponds more to the material and thoughts I would like to share.

My topic, briefly, is some of the problems that we—I mean the Czechoslovak Embassy—encounter in our information work here in the United States. Because the embassy is involved here, and because I shall refer on several occasions to my experience while performing official embassy duties. I would like to stress that what I am saying does not necessarily represent the official Czechoslovak Embassy or Government position and is to a very large degree only my personal interpretation of views and facts.

Let us consider first, in outline, some objective conditions that seem to determine to a great extent Czechoslovakia's position, her image, and her chances of presenting a clear picture of herself in the United States.

O As everyone is very well aware, Czechoslovakia is a small country in Central Europe. It is a socialist country and is closely allied with the Soviet Union and other socialist nations. This may sum up many Americans' total knowledge of the country.

· On the other hand, most Americans have, I assume, a pretty accurate idea of the size, political, social, and economic system of the United States, as well as of its foreign political and military affiliations. In short, your knowledge of your own country is naturally much more extensive.

· In the press attaché's particular field of information or—if you wish—propaganda, one must always, in any country, consider the specific features or characteristics of the local press, radio, television, and other information media. I shall consequently spend some time considering the American press in explaining how Czechoslovakia attempts to present information about itself.

Now to elaborate briefly on some of these objective "facts of life": The size of Czechoslovakia (a mere 14 million people, less than 50 thousand square miles) and the geographic distance between her and the United States account in themselves for the fact that people here in general know much less about Czechoslovakia than, say the Czechoslovaks do about the United States.

I am reminded of one incident that probably could illustrate this: Shortly after I came to Washington—it was in the summer of 1963—preparations were under way for the state visit to the United States of Marshall J. B. Tito, the President of Yugoslavia. You would be surprised to learn how many telephone calls *our* embassy received in connection with this visit, and these were often calls from journalists; that is, from people who might be supposed to be very well versed in geography and international politics.

In general people here in the United States do very often mix Yugoslavia and Czechoslovakia—the similarity of names is certainly partly responsible for this—and I am sure my Yugoslav colleague has often had a difficult time explaining how Jan Hus or Antonín Dvořák fit into the framework of Yugoslav national culture, just as we have when asked about Serbian, Croatian, Slovenian, or other writers, poets, or fighters.

I am not saying all this to support the oversimplified view classifying Americans as simple-minded or unsophisticated, although taking Yugoslavia for Czechoslovakia and vice versa may be compared to mixing Mexico with Brazil. On the contrary, I have found here as much sophistication and sometimes even more education than in Europe. I just want to show you that the order of values and the order of priorities are different here and in Czechoslovakia—and, as much as I regret it, I have to admit that it seems pretty difficult to convince the Americans that Czechoslovakia is the most important country in the world.

(In line with this, though, we would probably settle even for recognition as the most important country in Central Europe. This would be in line with our way of reporting on some of our achievements: whenever we build a bridge, we always look around for the nearest bigger bridge and then say something to the effect that the bridge just built is the biggest in a specific area—avoiding the area of the "nearest biggest." You, too, know the practice, as was demonstrated to me recently when I was staying in a downtown motor lodge in Philadelphia. The lodge was advertised as "World's Most Luxurious Motel in Downtown Philadelphia." I didn't have time to check if the owner was of Czechoslovak origin.) So, as you see, there are some problems and difficulties for which even a Czechoslovak press attaché cannot be held responsible.

As I said before, Czechoslovakia is a socialist country (or as you usually say, communist; I only wish we were that far). This certainly does present some problems to us in the United States. Every piece of information our embassy releases, every Czechoslovak film run in the States, and every book published here by us is an open invitation for a close scrutiny and may very easily be labeled "communist propaganda."

The trouble is that our views, ideas, and explanations are sometimes automatically rejected here simply because they originate from a "communist source," and their possible merits or demerits are not even discussed or tested. We acknowledge that a number of Americans have their doubts about socialism and that some of them simply don't like communism and do not want even to consider it as a possible alternative. This is as true as saying that only a few Czechoslovaks would think today about restoring capitalism, economically, politically, or socially. This should not, however, prevent us from learning about the other man, about his ideas and his country.

It is a sad fact that the cold war produced not only a number of misinterpretations and misrepresentation of socialist Czechoslovakia and the life of her people, but also brought about a situation that makes it fequently imperative to explain to a foreign audience even the basic facts about Czechoslovakia—to prove that it is a civilized and modern country and that the people over there do not wear horns. I know, and I am glad, that this state of affairs is changing and that it is changing for the better. Our political and ideological differences will, however, for as long as they exist, tempt some people to accept simple and distorted explanations instead of making a serious study.

Anticommunism is deeply embedded in the minds of some Americans, to an extent that often seems almost ridiculous to us. I remember an old lady from the Midwest who came to our embassy some time in 1965 with a group taking one of those many embassy tours that take place in Washington every year. This lady asked some questions about Czechoslovakia, admired the pictures and glass displayed, and after I answered some of her questions about the political system in Czechoslovakia, she said, "But you are not a Communist, are you?" When I told her I was, she said she could not believe it and that I must be joking. "You look quite normal to me," she added. I was certainly very much flattered that at least somebody thought I was normal, and I have always used this since as an argument with my wife and friends who sometimes insist I am not in my right mind.

I know that this old—and altogether very pleasant and polite —lady is not representative of a cross section of American ideas about the communists and that she does not symbolize the thinking of the younger generation of Americans. However, she pointed quite clearly to one of the most urgent and difficult tasks we have in our information work here: to prove to the American people that we are normal, that we are sincerely interested in peace, trade, and technical and scientific cooperation as well as in exchanging the best achievements in culture and education. You will probably agree with me that this is not easy to accomplish when so many people and so many relics of the past are still against us; but we will never stop trying, and we hope that eventually the political and ideological factors will cease to play the overriding and most important role in the American approach to Czechoslovakia. As I indicated before, this may be happening now.

No embassy can carry alone the burden of information about

its country. Even the big embassies that can afford to pay considerable amounts of money to various public relations firms have no illusions about the effectiveness and limitations of information the embassy disseminates. Too, people here, like everywhere, do not rely for their daily information on embassy bulletins and press releases. They read newspapers, listen to the radio and television, and mostly believe in what they learn from these sources. The question is, therefore, how to reach the American press, and, further, how not only to make our information available to it, but also how to make our information actually appear in it. I confess that after spending almost four years in this country, I have no single answer ready. The American press, which looked a puzzle to me when I arrived here in 1963, does not seem to be such a puzzle any longer—but to say that this helps very much would be an overstatement. Besides the ideological element that is certainly very important here, there are some other features about the American press that should always be considered by us—as I see it.

First, the American press deals, on the whole, with a substantially different reader from that of our press. What concerns us most is the different approach to foreign policy issues; such issues seem to be of primary importance to the vast majority of educated readership in Czechoslovakia, while most American readers —so it seems to me—look for more pragmatic and practical issues. This difference in reader interest certainly shows very distinctly in the papers themselves, for example, in the front-page stories about accidents, and so on. It could be explained by different traditions and different fears: the fate of Czechoslovakia very often depended on somebody else's decision; for example, the Czechs and Slovaks had to look for outside help in fighting for independence or in fighting against Hitler. There is also the old Central European tradition of "beer politics" so colorfully depicted by Hašek in his *Good Soldier Schweik,* where Schweik presents his table companion Bretschneider, who is a police agent, with solutions that would easily dispose of the gravest problems and troubles of the Austro-Hungarian monarchy. You are probably familiar with the practical result of this theorizing: that Schweik got a chance for a rather close and intensive study of the Austro-Hungarian police and judicial systems.

Second, the American press is essentially local. Even the *New*

York Times or the *Washington Post* cannot justly claim to be national newspapers. What is news in Washington is not necessarily—and, it seems to me, more often is not—news in Los Angeles, or even in Baltimore. Only the magazines and probably the television networks compensate for the role of a national newspaper or newspapers to which we are accustomed in Czechoslovakia. Thus much of the publicity you may have here may easily be confined to one area only—with very little chance to reach, undistorted, all the localities in the States.

Third, the American press is expensive, or, to be more exact, publicity is expensive. We certainly cannot afford to spend $75,000 or so twice a year to have a special commercial travel section in a leading newspaper, or to pay hundreds of dollars to publicists to write articles that may not be published at all.

Fourth, the American press is essentially self-reliant. At least the big and important papers prefer to work with staff reporters rather than free-lancers, and generally very little material of outside origin appears in the daily press here. (I exclude prepaid news services and syndicated columnists, etc.; they are all parts of an existing press establishment.) The American press claims to be independent, strictly refusing, therefore, any foreign embassy or government material.

These, briefly, are my observations as to the characteristics of the American press. As you can see, many of them make it difficult for us to approach the press directly with our material and information, and I am sure that nobody could accuse us of seeking inroads to subvert this colossus. Beside the objective limitations, we must always bear in mind that an embassy is not an information or propaganda center, that its duties and activities are limited by its diplomatic status, and that the embassy can present only the official government view and thus may not always serve as the best source of information for the newspaperman.

What can we do, then, to help promote our interests in the United States?

An easy way to get into the news is to do something wrong or to do something that disagrees with the policies of this country. For different reasons that are not directly connected with the subject of this collection of discussions, we cannot help disagreeing with the United States on a number of issues. It is the duty of our embassy to explain to the press—and to anybody asking— the reasons for our policies and the motivation for our position. We welcome such inquiries, and I must say that on several occasions we have succeeded in at least having our views quoted. Some of the political factors are still responsible for the fact that, say, failure to achieve a certain economic objective gets much more publicity here than successful achievement of 10 planned or unplanned targets. The most effective way of fighting this bias is certainly to avoid making mistakes, but this is not always possible. Therefore what we do is recognize our mistakes openly and fairly; if you could read the Czechoslovak press and the official statements in it, you would find that it is full of frank and detailed analysis of economic and even political shortcomings or mistakes. We try to do the same here, whenever our view on these things is being sought by the press.

We also supply the press—and anybody interested—with documentation, information brochures, and other "propaganda" material. In fact, we receive so many requests now that our meager supply of information material cannot cope with them. We receive—and sometimes answer—letters from students who not only want material, but write something like this: "Dear Sir, next week I am to present a paper on Czechoslovak relations with Cambodia. In my work I have to cover the following subjects . . ." and down goes a long list of issues that should be treated, then . . . "I hope that you can send me your documented answers to these questions as soon as possible, in view of the fact that I must present my paper next week. . . ." We also receive questions on the frequency of eucalyptuses in Southern Slovakia, on the behavior of bees in the Bohemian forests, and others asking what is the difference between the bohemians in Greenwich Village and the Bohemians in Bohemia (the answer is none— they both drink too much). We try our best to answer as many of the letters as we can, but if we don't answer yours, do not be angry at us.

An important part of our embassy's job here is assisting American journalists in their travel plans for Czechoslovakia. In cooperation with the Press Office of the Foreign Ministry in Prague and with other institutions and organizations there, we try to give journalists the chance to meet interesting people and to see places in which they are interested. We suggest what may be worth seeing in addition to a journalist's own plan. I must say that we welcome American journalists in Czechoslovakia and we are glad when they come. We know that very often they will write critically about their impressions, but we also believe that through this writing Czechoslovakia will become better known to the Americans. We sincerely hope that their articles will be more objective and more favorable to Czechoslovakia than some of them used to be in the past. It is a pity that no permanent American correspondent has been stationed in Prague; you will agree that nothing can replace an experience of a prolonged stay in the country you are writing about.

We certainly do a number of other things in public relations and information: for instance, we send speakers to universities and schools, receive student groups, and distribute some films. On the whole, we are pretty busy. What I want to illustrate by all this is that dealing with press and public relations is sometimes a pretty hard job; that it may be even bureaucratic, involving quite a lot of paperwork; that in our work we encounter a number of limitations, both objective and subjective; and that we have to bear them always in mind when dealing with the American press or directly with the American public. But it is still exciting because explaining your own country and your own ideas and way of life to somebody who does not always see them the way you do is always exciting, and instructive for both parties involved.

Now let me add something on real promotion. I don't know to what extent it has come out clearly from what I have already written, but one of the conclusions should be that no public image of a country could be supported and installed firmly without her deserving this image. On the other hand, you cannot forever destroy the image of a country by propaganda only. Sooner or later somebody will ask you to produce proof.

From this point of view, the biggest promotion effort has been under way in Czechoslovakia for years. It is an effort to build Czechoslovakia into a strong, economically sound, and socially just Socialist Republic.

We have a number of things we can be proud of: the over-all

industrial production in Czechoslovakia in 1965 was almost five times bigger than that of the year 1937, with the national income increased over 2.6 times. Even our foes have to agree that we have one of the best systems of health and social security (all medical expenses paid, all treatment free), a good system of education (free to the highest level), reasonable housing policy, and so on. As most people probably know, we are now undergoing a far-reaching reform of economic management that should further increase the vitality of our economy. In recent years we have been quite successful in the cultural field; I am glad that, for example, Czechoslovak films did finally find their way to the American market, and I sincerely believe that anybody seeing "The Shop on Main Street," "The Loves of a Blonde," "The Diamonds of Night," or any other good Czechoslovak film could no longer see Czechoslovakia as a dull, oppressive, and hostile country as it was pictured by the anticommunist cold war propaganda.

And our biggest stake is obviously with the many thousands of foreigners—among them about 40,000 American visitors in 1966—who come to Czechoslovakia every year and see for themselves. Needless to say, they find many things to complain about—after all, we do not make any secret of our drawbacks and insufficiencies— but they also see more places and things to love.

11

From Red Square to Pennsylvania Avenue

YURI I. BOBRAKOV
PRESS ATTACHÉ
EMBASSY OF THE U.S.S.R.

YURI IVANOVITCH BOBRAKOV is a northerner, from Leningrad. When he was eight years old his father, an engineer, moved the family to Moscow. Mr. Bobrakov studied political economy at Moscow University, then taught as a professor of economics before switching to journalism as an economic observer for APN (Novosti), Russia's second news agency.

In 1963 Mr. Bobrakov was offered a position with the Soviet Embassy in Washington, which he says he accepted because "I had never had an assignment in other countries. It was a chance to learn about the United States." Accompanying him to Washington were his wife (an artist well known in diplomatic circles) and his nine-year-old daughter. Although he holds the diplomatic rank of Second Secretary, he says he does not consider himself a career diplomat.

Mr. Bobrakov has written several books, but after he came to Washington he found he had less time to write. His recent publications include an article on "Law and Contemporary Problems" for Duke University.

DEFINITIONS are, by their own nature, limited. In defining the embassy press attaché we may describe him as a diplomatic official dealing with the press. Such a definition, although correct in essence, is not quite complete.

Our job resembles that of a housewife: we work all day, but there is always some work still undone. Dealing directly with the press is only part of our daily routine. For instance, press attachés are often called upon to speak not only to press people, but to civic groups, universities, religious groups, and so on. We have our bureaucratic, red-tape jobs such as, in my embassy, helping American correspondents assigned to Moscow to get their papers in order, and we also sometimes have unexpected jobs such as answering phone calls from the wives of correspondents who ask, "Listen, if I'm going to Moscow with my husband, there are things I need to know. How about beauty salons in the U.S.S.R.? What kind of clothing should I take?" I find these tough to answer. My wife usually has to help me out.

Nor is the press attaché's job done when the day ends. A press attaché, being a member of the diplomatic corps, also must participate in an after-hours social life. This is something familiar to Washington journalists, who are always broadly represented at the diplomatic events taking place in the U.S. capital.

For all that we are busy, and sometimes think we are popular, until early in 1967 the press attaché was an underprivileged person. In Washington members of practically every profession or walk of life have an organization, a social club to which they can belong. The press attachés did not. Se we decided we would get together and upgrade our status to that of the normal Washington resident by organizing a social club. In February 1967 we had an inaugural lunch, with White House Press Secretary George Christian delivering the inaugural address. We hoped this club would allow us to exchange bureaucratic news and to get to know each other a little better, and, although it is still in its babyhood, it shows promise of becoming a well-established institution. In order to reach a successful maturity the "club" is now passing through what can be called its "teenageship." I am a hope addict. I hope the club will flourish and make progress.

Speaking seriously of the job of a press attaché and the many responsibilities associated with this position, it is necessary to emphasize one thing that has an important meaning in the fulfillment of an attaché's everyday duties. A press attaché is an avid reader, and, quite naturally, he pays special attention to material in the local press that is related to his country and its policy, economy, culture, history, and current events—the life of its people.

During my four years in Washington I have read innumerable columns, editorials, comments in American newspapers, magazine articles, to say nothing of the many different books by different authors that appear on the book market. There are many points on which I might express my views concerning the history and life of my country as covered by the American press.

It is actually impossible to embrace the whole subject; its spaciousness makes it something "unembraceable." Therefore I should like to limit myself to the subject that, with its advent, grew increasingly closer to the heart of every person in my country—the fiftieth anniversary of the Great October Socialist Revolution in Russia.

The nearer the anniversary day of November 7, 1967, came, the more comments appeared on the pages of the American press. With every month this process developed by geometrical progression. That would have been welcome if it were really an unbiased description of what happened in Russia 50 years ago, but from what was being published while this chapter was in the writing stage, some trends and tendencies had already developed that in my opinion were anything but an impartial assessment. I would not take upon myself the task of total evaluation of these tendencies, but at least some comments, in my view, are necessary.

Take the question of the history of the October Revolution.

In my opinion there was and is a tendency to present the victory of the revolution as something accidental, as a "Bolshevik conspiracy," as a miscarriage of history rather than the logical result of social development. In effect, such a presentation is not something new; for years it had been propagated by such bankrupt politicians of the Russian scene as P. Miljukov, V. Chernov, A. Kerensky, and others. If we look at the comments in some American newspapers, only a very few days after the revolution, we see that the thesis of the "accidental" nature of the October Revolution was also inherent there. This is what the *New York Tribune* wrote about the revolution in its issue of November 9, 1917:

"The Bolshevik party in power assuming the responsibility of a government is a helpless and futile anomaly. . . . To speak of a government by such a faction is a palpable absurdity. Even in Russia it is impossible . . . . Their collapse is inevitable and when it comes, whether in a few days or in a fortnight, Russia will have been purged of the poison which has turned democracy into a nightmare."

The *Baltimore Sun,* in its editorial on November 11, 1917, made the following comment:

"The program of these maximum radicals [Bolsheviks] has two large items—an immediate peace, and the immediate handing over of the large proprietorial lands to the peasants.

"That no stable government can be founded upon such a political platform is apparent on thoughtful minds . . . ."

As history has convincingly shown, such "thoughtful" predictions did not come true.

History witnessed the rise and fall of monarchies in the ancient East, the republics of ancient Greece, the Roman and Byzantine empires, medieval feudal states, absolute monarchies, bourgeois democracies, and colonial empires. Historically, 50 years is not a long time. History knows nations and civilizations that existed for hundreds and even thousands of years. By this measure the Soviet country is very young. But the existence of the Soviet state, born in October 1917, has rendered an immeasurable influence on world history.

The October Socialist Revolution not only opened up a new era in the life of more than 130 nations and peoples inhabiting our country; it gave a great impetus to social progress, it brought about a sort of chain reaction that changed the face of the modern world.

It is said that in order to see the mountain better, one should look at it from a distance; but some people, even at a distance of 50 years, fail to see the meaning of the event that took place at that time.

I cannot help smiling at the naïveté of the statements similar, for example, to those in the *U.S. News and World Report* of March 13, 1967, describing the October Revolution as a "sharp, violent military coup," linked with the hopes of the German High Command to "stir up enough trouble to knock Russia out of the first World War."

The October Revolution was an organic result of the historical development of the economic and political forces in Russia, of the sharpening of the social contradictions within Russian society.

The revolution was prepared by years of struggle by the working masses of Russia for liberation from the tsarist and capitalist exploitation. The Communist Party (Bolsheviks) correctly understood the trends of history and the aspirations of the people's masses, and energetically worked for their fulfillment. It was for this reason that it was capable of assuming the leadership and carrying the revolution toward victory. The February Revolution, which preceded the October Revolution by seven months, also took place as a result of the revolutionary struggle of the masses, in which the leading role belonged to the Bolshevik party.

In some recent comments of the American press on the February Revolution, I saw a definite attempt to "excommunicate" the Bolsheviks from the revolution.

The *New York Times* (March 13, 1967) wrote:

"Conspirators of various political shades had been working in Russia for a century to bring about the revolution. Yet it was not the conspirators who started the revolution; it was the women. They needed bread. This was a revolution without revolutionists."

Again the words "conspiracy," "conspirators"—it looks like a sort of "conspiratorial obsession." Concerning the role of the Bolsheviks in the revolution, the author of the *Times* piece declared that "they had played virtually no role in bringing it about."

The *Washington Evening Star* in its March 12, 1967, issue, commented in the same vein: "As for the Bolsheviks, they were caught entirely by surprise. They did not even play a minor role in the popular revolution." Such theory on the February Revolution is very similar to that exercised by Mensheviks and Socialist-Revolutionaries, who also tried hard to excommunicate the Bolsheviks from the revolution.

It needs hardly to be said that such versions of the role of the Bolshevik party in the revolution bear no resemblance to the facts.

The Bolsheviks were the only party that systematically and consistently prepared the masses for a decisive battle with the regime. Late in 1916 the Russian Bureau instructed the Petrograd and Moscow Party Committees to organize mass demonstrations culminating in a general strike: in other words, to prepare for open war against tsarism, for the transition from scattered economical and political actions to organized mass political struggle. At factory meetings, in leaflets, and through other media, the Bolsheviks called for a decisive battle. One such leaflet, issued by the Petrograd Committee, read:

"We must more and more powerfully swing the pendulum of the revolution. From economic struggle against capitalism in the factories the movement must grow into a broad political struggle, a struggle for power, into civil war."

However, owing to a number of factors, the February Revolution carried out by the workers and peasants did not result in the establishment of a genuine people's government.

It was not long before the people realized the Provisional Government was merely continuing the foreign and domestic policies of the tsar. The people wanted peace, but were being made to continue the war. The peasants wanted land, but the government did not dare to encroach on the big landed estates. The workers demanded bread, but the food shortage was becoming worse every day. Russia was rapidly sliding into economic ruin.

For the Russia of 1917, socialism was the only way out of the horrors of war, famine, and economic chaos. The October Revolution consummated the work begun in February.

There have been many comments in the American press to the effect that the February Revolution was the "victory of democracy" and the October Revolution "the destruction of democracy."

By overthrowing tsarism, the people won a bourgeois-democratic system. But the bourgeoisie was incapable of solving even a single one of the many tasks posed by the revolution.

The Soviet Government, established in 1917, brought the people peace and freedom from exploitation and opened up new vistas for the future. Once masters of the country, the people displayed miracles of heroism in defending it against its many foes. The civil war was a vast referendum in which the people voted for Soviet power as the embodiment of their hopes and aspirations.

The proponents of the "accidental" nature of the October Revolution do not spare their efforts in accusing the Communist Party of undemocratic means of attaining power, of pushing aside other political parties that had lawful rights of holding the political leadership of the country.

I think a short excursion into history might be helpful in casting light on the situation and establishing the real picture of the political struggles of the time.

After the overthrow of the monarchy in February 1917, all political parties had an opportunity to advance if their programs and political policies met the demands of the people; these demands were focused on three words: peace, bread, and freedom.

Did the Socialist-Revolutionary Party or the Mensheviks—the two opponents of the Bolshevik Party in the struggle for power —meet the popular demands?

The Socialist-Revolutionaries, as is well known, linked their destiny with the Provisional Government. Their leader, Alexander Kerensky, made a career in this government and became a premier. By associating themselves with the Provisional Government, the Socialist-Revolutionaries discredited themselves in the minds of the people.

The Mensheviks (the right wing of the Russian Social-Democratic Labor Party) did not believe that the Socialist Revolution could triumph in the economically backward Russia. They supported the Provisional Government's policy of continuing the war. This stand could not gain popularity for the Mensheviks with the large masses of Russian people.

In contradiction to the political programs of the Socialist-Revolutionaries and the Mensheviks, the program of the Communists met the vital needs and aspirations of the toiling population: it desired the immediate withdrawal of Russia from the war, the parceling of landed estates out to the peasants, and the transfer of political power to the Soviets.

By the very course of events, the popularity of the Communist Party with the masses grew day by day, while the Socialist-Revolutionaries and the Mensheviks were losing their support. This did not happen because of the viciousness of the Communists. It was the Communists who were entrusted by the All-Russia Congress of Soviets, which represented the majority of the Russian population, with the formation of the first Soviet government.

The Communists did not push aside the Socialist-Revolutionaries and the Mensheviks, but decided to give them their chance and invited them to join the government. This proposal, as is known, was turned down. The leftist Socialist-Revolutionaries later accepted Lenin's proposal and got seven ministerial posts (People's Commissars, as they were called at that time).

As history gives proof, the Communist Party did not push aside its opponent parties, but invited them into the government. The collaboration did not last long, however. In a few months' time the Socialist-Revolutionaries staged an armed revolt against the Soviet power. The Socialist-Revolutionaries and the Mensheviks allied themselves with the counterrevolutionary forces and thus doomed themselves to failure. These parties were ultimately wiped from the political scene, not because of Communist violence, but because their policies were opposed to the interests of the people of Russia. This, I think, should be clear to any unbiased person who is acquainted with the facts of Russian history.

One of the contentions of the critics of the Great October Socialist Revolution is that the Communists failed to win the support of the Russian intelligentsia, which allegedly refused to accept the revolution and came out against it. The facts of history convincingly disprove these contentions. A large part of the intelligentsia, who took the destiny of the country to heart, participated in the political struggle of the proletariat. They came to realize that the ideals of the Communist Party were directly associated with the promotion of progress and prosperity in the country.

Of course, there were a good many intellectuals who found themselves lost in the storms of the early period of the revolution. The Communist Party did everything possible to help the old intelligentsia to find its place in the revolutionary process, and this purposeful policy had a beneficial effect on the old intelligentsia. It is sufficient to say that even in the years of the civil war the Soviet power secured extensive support among them; by the middle of August 1920, some 50,000 former officers and generals assumed important posts in the Red Army. Tens of thousands of engineers, technicians, and other specialists worked in the national economy. The party displayed the greatest tact and patience toward the intelligentsia. "Unless our leading institutions," Lenin urged, "that is, the Communist Party, the Soviet government, and the trade unions, come to the point where they will guard, as the apple of their eye, every specialist working conscientiously, competently, and lovingly, even if he is totally alien to communist ideology, there can be no talk of any serious successes in socialist construction." The old intelligentsia did find its place in the new society and brought its knowledge to the service of the socialist construction.

For half a century the Soviet power has been in existence in our country. During this time gigantic changes have taken place, the principal result being the new socialist society, entering the stage of its maturity, which leads to the construction of the communist society.

I shall not resort to statistics—I presume that the knowledge of the fact that the U.S.S.R. is a great industrial power has long ago become a part of the modern way of life.

At present a great emphasis in my country is made on the successful materialization of the economic reform, aimed at bringing methods of economic management into conformity with the level attained in social development, at accelerating scientific and technical progress in the economy, and at creating the production apparatus of communist society.

I read quite a number of comments in the American press on the economic reform in our country and, speaking frankly, I could not keep from smiling at the allegations "free-enterprise revolution," "creeping capitalism," and the like.

Castles in the air can be comfortable until you step out the door. The contentions of transformation of the socialist economy in the U.S.S.R. have nothing to do with reality and for this reason cannot be treated seriously. The economic reform in my country is a socialist measure based on the socialist economic principles and aimed at the further perfecting of the mechanism of the socialist economy, and its development toward communist goals.

The fiftieth anniversary of the October Revolution was also the fiftieth anniversary of the Soviet foreign policy, which began its history with the Decree on Peace adopted by the Second All-Russia Congress of Soviets on November 8, 1917. The decree contained an appeal to all the belligerent countries to begin negotiations for the cessation of the war and the conclusion of a just, democratic peace without annexations and contributions. It was a virtual proclamation of the idea of the possibility of coexistence of states that represent different social systems.

The Soviet foreign policy, born in October 1917, has always been consistent in its aims of providing for peaceful conditions for the construction of socialism and communism, of strengthening the principles of peaceful coexistence, and in its efforts to promote peace in the world.

12

Taiwan, Bastion of the Orient

RICHARD L. JEN
PRESS COUNSELOR
EMBASSY OF THE REPUBLIC OF CHINA

RICHARD L. JEN, Press Counselor of the Embassy of the Republic of China, was born in Tientsin, China, in 1907. He was educated at Yenching University in Peking, and at the School of Journalism of the University of Washington in Seattle.

Mr. Jen has a long and active record as a newspaperman and foreign correspondent before joining his government's embassy in Washington in 1963. He was news editor of the *Peking Chronicle* from 1931 to 1933; chief of the English News Department for the Central News Agency in Tientsin, Nanking, and Shanghai from 1933 to 1937; editor of the *China Fortnightly* in Hong Kong from 1938 to 1939; Honk Kong bureau chief for Central News Agency from 1939 to 1941.

For the next 21 years (1942 through 1963) he was a foreign correspondent for Central News Agency, serving as chief of the bureaus in India, London, Pacific Coast-USA, and Washington, D.C. He has covered such stories as the organizational session of the United Nations in London, the first General Assembly Session of the United Nations in London, Gandhi's nonviolent resistance movement in India during World War II, the European Peace Conference in Paris at the end of World War II, atomic bomb tests in Nevada, the Japanese Peace Conference in San Francisco, Democratic and Republican Party conventions; and he has served as White House and State Department correspondent.

In 1963 he joined the Chinese Embassy in Washington. He served as Press Secretary to Madame Chiang Kai-shek during her 1965-1966 tour of the United States.

IT PROBABLY seems unbelievable to you whose history goes back only about two centuries that as early as 2250 years ago public relations as a concept of goodwill building was known to China.

It was the news-studded period of the Warring States in China, about 300 B.C. It was a transitional period in Chinese history, when royal authority was on the decline and political power rested in the hands of the feudal lords. It was an era when a political system flourished under which feudal lords or the nobility tried to recruit, by every means possible, the services of men with assorted talents and ideas.

An ancient version of the first Chinese public relations expert was recorded in the history of the Ch'i Dynasty. The Prime Minister, Meng Ch'ang-chun, had assembled in his employ as many as 3000 advisers gifted in various and many fields. Numbered among these counselors was one Feng Huan, a man with a creative mind whose primary duty was as indefinite as it was indefinable, somewhat equivalent to what may be known today as a troubleshooter.

There came a year when Feng was assigned the chore of assessing and collecting taxes and debts from the tenanted peasants on Lord Meng's feudal estates.

His brain apparently working the same way the late Mr. Ivy Lee's was functioning in relation to John D. Rockefeller, Sr., Mr. Feng immediately saw in his new job a fertile field for image projection.

Unlike Mr. Ivy Lee's time, however, there were no newspapers in those days in China. Instead of adjusting and collecting taxes and debts for his master, Feng launched a publicity campaign by word-of-mouth about a massive rally to be held, and at the appointed day and hour staged a public burning of all the promissory notes and loan contracts, thus engraving an invisible but indelible headline in the head and mind of every inhabitant of the town—Lord Meng was not only a man of wealth and power but a man of heart and compassion as well.

It would be an understatement to say that the Honorable Meng was unhappy about his adviser's inexplicably fantastic behavior. As a matter of fact, he was furious over the loss of a small fortune. Later on, however, he realized that what was due his publicity adviser was not punishment but gratitude. Not long afterwards, for reasons unrecorded in the history books, Lord Meng was fired by the Emperor. However, when Meng, downcast, returned to his home town, lo and behold, he was not faced with disgrace; the entire populace of the city rolled out the red carpet to give him a hero's welcome. The Emperor, told of the high popularity rating his ousted Prime Minister enjoyed among the people, recalled him to the service of the Court and appointed him to an even higher position.

Let me emphasize here that the citing of this story about Feng Huan, predating Ivy Lee by 2000 years, does not constitute a claim that China by now must be far advanced in the field of public relations. On the contrary, she is just an infant. Like so many of our inventions, such as firecrackers and explosives, the art of paper-making, and the printing press, the art of publicity was never nurtured until the West demonstrated its necessity. As a science or a technique, public relations has been a relatively recent development, in government or in industry.

As a matter of fact, the Chinese Government failed to see the importance of public relations as a bridge between China and public opinion abroad until Japan let loose the full force of its military juggernaut on Shanghai and the mainland in full-fledged aggression. Chinese officialdom had thought with puritan naïveté that our just cause was sufficient in itself to induce a favorable press.

It was not until the end of 1937, when stories of the infamous Rape of Nanking were interpreted abroad as "Chinese inventions" designed to obtain foreign sympathy, that the Government decided to set up a Ministry of Information. Dr. Hollington

Tong, an American-trained veteran newspaperman, was picked to be the Vice-Minister of Information in charge of international publicity. Dr. Tong, familiarly known to hundreds of American newsmen as "Holly," was later to become Chinese Ambassador to the United States. China's first bona fide foreign correspondent was not sent to the United States till 1940, short of a year before the eruption of Pearl Harbor.

Though the Government was now aware of the critical urgency of telling China's story to the world, they were still woefully ignorant of the high price tags for an information program. Dr. Tong, in his book *China and the World Press,* tells the pathetic story that in 1938, the second year of Japan's invasion of China, only 3000 U.S. dollars were appropriated to run his international publicity program.

Things have changed since then, especially after the late 1940's, when the Republic of China reached the nadir of despair in the world press. The Communists on the mainland were riding high, and enjoyed a good press in the United States, aided and abetted by communist propaganda subtly filtered through the pens and mouths of fellow travellers. In the early 1950's, with our Government temporarily moved to Taiwan and its shoulders set to the wheel, so to speak, the function of public relations gained new importance. It has now been accepted as an integral part of government.

A full-fledged agency to handle and run the country's overseas public relations and information program was set up, with a moderately respectable (never adequate) budget of its own. Since 1958 the same name has been used for this agency: the Government Information Office; it is directly under the Executive Yuan (the Cabinet), and its Director (now Mr. James Wei, an oldtimer in the newspaper business) enjoys sub-Cabinet status. Press attachés began to be assigned to various embassies (GIO now has 17 overseas missions), thus making public relations an indispensable dimension of diplomacy.

The primary function of the Government Information Office, as is expected, is to tell the story of the Republic of China, to explain China in all its aspects, its culture, its philosophy, its government, its people, and its policy. Another function is to help create a favorable atmosphere abroad for a better understanding of China's progress and policies and to promote good-will between the Republic of China and other friendly countries.

Compared with the magnitude of the information program of the United States Information Agency, which has an annual budget of $170 million, the Chinese GIO budget is indeed minimally modest. However, with its limited funds, the Government Information Office has chosen to perform its function by laying greater stress on an information program than on public relations promotional campaigns. On the theory that a good drummer does not need an oversized drumstick, its genuineness speaking for itself, the GIO devotes virtually its entire resources to the dissemination of factual information on what the Republic of China has been and is doing, with military and economic aid from the United States, in its many-faceted nation-building program, as an eventual model for all China.

This information program is conducted through films, books, pamphlets, brochures and folders, slides, posters, magazines, and pictures. Publications produced in 1966, in 60 different titles and printed in seven foreign languages—English, French, Spanish, Japanese, German, Arabic, and Thai—totaled 1,250,000. These were distributed in 11 countries in Latin America, two in the North American Continent, eight in Asia, and in Australia and New Zealand. Other informational output included nine documentary films, 180 newsreels in three foreign languages, 620 tapes in 18 foreign languages, 24 television films in English, French, and Spanish, and 100,000 news photos, both black-and-white and color.

The information bridge from China to the United States is a two-lane bridge. First, the GIO seeks to channel its information and news to this country through the foreign press corps stationed in Taipei, which today has 25 service and newspaper representations, of which 11 are American, including AP, UPI, NBC-TV, CBS, Time-Life, Newsweek, MGM, and Movietone News. Besides news releases and communiqués issued by the Foreign Office and the Ministry of National Defense, the GIO holds regular weekly press conferences. In 1965, for example, 46 regular and 16 special press conferences were held, and 981 news bulletins issued. In addition to facilitating spot news coverage by the foreign press corps the GIO distributes, through a contract signed with a news syndicate in 1962, press features on free China as the free world's bastion of the Pacific, its development, its activities, and its plans.

Second, paralleling the information program emanating from our home base, is GIO's overseas arm. Whatever titles we hold— press counselors, press attachés, or information officers—we as overseas public relations representatives are only part of its transmission belt, just as USIS missions overseas are to your U.S. Information Agency in Washington. The GIO maintains three offices in the United States; in Washington, New York, and San Francisco. Technically the three offices have different functions, New York being predominantly a production and distribution center and San Francisco largely operative in the Western States; the objectives of the three are essentially identical: to provide information to the press and public about the Republic of China, to make the facts and truths known to as wide an audience as possible, by radio, film, television, pictures, and the printed word.

Specifically, as Press Counselor of the Chinese Embassy, what do I and my office do in Washington? Our functions are primarily five: (a) we act as the spokesman of the embassy and therefore of the Chinese Government; (b) we serve as the public relations adviser for the embassy as well as VIP vistors from free China; (c) we double as a sort of tourist agent; (d) we distribute GIO publications and other informational materials from Taipei; and (e) we strive our best to play, by American public acclamation, the role of an encylopedic tutor on China and things Chinese.

Having been a practicing newspaperman for nearly 30 years, I found myself, nevertheless, a neophyte in publicity or public relations work when I was appointed to my present position as Press Counselor of the Embassy in 1963, although the two fields seem on the surface to be rather similar. On the other hand, perhaps because I was active newspaperman myself for many years, I found the "spokesmanship" part of my job at once the easiest and the most difficult.

It is easiest because we always put ourselves in the position of the newsmen seeking information, trying our best to help them do their job. In that context, we tell them as much as we know.

The news may be favorable or unfavorable, but we like to give all the facts and the truths as we have them and as we see them. We like to be factually accurate and straightforward.

How do we prepare ourselves for the "spokesmanship" assignment? To keep ourselves absolutely abreast of what is happening at home, we do an enormous amount of reading, both in Chinese and English. First, we read the daily news file cabled to our offices from Taipei, everything that Taipei judges to be important and timely. Then we pore over the "guidelines" and background materials on various news events that our GIO head office and our Foreign Office in Taipei send us several times a week. We read all the Chinese newspapers and news magazines that are airmailed to us from Taipei every two or three days.

Outside of straight news or anything we cannot handle, we fall back on the Ambassador. Whenever any major news breaks, such as Red China's nuclear detonation, or Senator Robert Kennedy's advocacy of closer contacts with Peiping, we anticipate queries from the press for our reaction. We ask the Ambassador in advance for a prepared statement. The moment the phone rings, from the first inquisitive reporter, we simply read the ready-made statement, and the inquiring newsman is usually satisfied when told he can quote the Ambassador.

Sometimes, of course, the newsman is not satisfied with simply a direct statement of reaction. When he is doing an in-depth probe of a news development, such as the current question of "what's really happening" on mainland China, we arrange for him to interview the Ambassador, normally within the day if the Ambassador is in town.

Occasionally, you can sense the tone of a hostile reporter going after a specially slanted angle. Even then, if he asks to talk to the Ambassador, we normally do not refuse to transmit his request. We realize that if an ambassador understands the importance of good press relations he will not turn down such a request, even at the risk of an occasional critical article.

There are, of course, some ambassadors who act as their own press secretaries, like some American presidents who act as their own secretaries of state. They are so accessible to the press that they take telephone calls themselves, and correspondents are able to talk to them directly, without an appointment arranged beforehand by their press secretaries. Some top-notch reporters and columnists are fond of boasting that they get their diplomatic "dope" from "the horse's mouth" so to speak, instead of distilled news and views from the lowly press officers.

The dilemma sometimes arises that when an ambassador makes himself instantly available to any and all reporters among the press corps, he runs the risk of being misquoted or misinterpreted, occasionally leaving embarrassing consequences beyond the control of his press officer after other reporters have picked up the distorted quotes.

What we are really up against—which is a most formidable problem—are the chronic prejudice-peddling anti-Nationalist writers who, forever harking back to the 1940's, unceasingly echo and parrot a wide variety of distortions and myths about us. The inherent seriousness of this problem is that a canard or a half-truth, if repeated often enough, passes through reporters' typewriters as historical fact.

The book *Formosa Betrayed*, by George Kerr, a wartime Naval reserve officer, is a good random example. Kerr repeats the canard about the so-called February 28, 1947, incident as being a "massacre." He freely and liberally exaggerates the figures of those killed as between 5000 and 20,000. Appearing to be "documenting" his charges, he cites no more specific sources than the statement or account of "one foreigner" or "one eyewitness." Our figures are that not more than 550 were killed in that unfortunate incident.

The gross inaccuracy of Kerr's book can be gauged by the accumulated inaccuracies of many occurrences passed as facts. On page 298, for instance, Kerr states categorically that "Gan Kin-en, owner and director of important mining interests, was seized and killed" during the incident.

Not long after the book made its appearance, the same Gan Kin-en wrote a letter to the press, not from heaven, but from Taipei, disclaiming the obituary of Kerr's authorship. "I was not seized by the Government forces in that incident," Gan said. "I certainly was not killed as I am still very much alive. As to my mining interests, they have been developing steadily in the past twenty years as a result of the Government's policy of encouragement to private enterprise on the island. I am now the President of Taiyang Mining Corp."

The difficulty of dealing with irresponsible writing and reckless criticism, I suspect, confronts similarly every government spokesman, irrespective of nationality. Robert J. Manning, when he was Assistant Secretary of State for Public Affairs, expressed this thought which I share, in a Washington speech on March 13, 1964. "It is no coincidence," Manning said, "that with rare exceptions the writers who regularly produce the most startling accusations about the State Department do not call my office or any other section of the department to ask questions or check conclusions. Apparently, they feel their concoctions will clang more loudly if not muted by the facts."

In the field of public relations per se, one of the "musts" of an embassy press officer is to cultivate the Washington press corps. However, as the press fraternity in the nation's capital— at once the most influential and most sophisticated group found anywhere—totals over 3000, any attempt to get even remotely acquainted with half of them would be next to impossible. Under these circumstances, we can only concentrate our cultivation with that group whose beat is Far Eastern affairs, be they wire-service men, local newspaper reporters, columnists, radio and television commentators, magazine writers, or freelancers. This selective method, from our own experiences, has proved to be practical, effective, and mutually beneficial, making accessibility mutually available whenever some major news breaks that has a China angle. Take the recent case of the Washington visit of our Vice President and Prime Minister, Mr. C. K. Yen. The "Far East" correspondents of the American and foreign wire services, including AP, UPI, Reuters, Agence France-Presse, the Copley News Service, and reporters of Washington newspapers all made themselves available at the embassy press office for advance texts of his speech several hours before he was to address the National Press Club. The news was already on the tickers when Mr. Yen started to speak.

Secondarily, we try to maintain contact with the diplomatic correspondents and society reporters who cover Embassy Row.

Besides the Far East reporters, these are the newsmen who we invite to our embassy receptions and other diplomatic functions. I mention this, not because we think they are gluttonous gourmets of exotic Oriental foods, but because the Washington press is unique among world capitals in one journalistic peculiarity. Practically all diplomatic news is found, not in the main news pages, but in the women's pages. This accounts for the half-humorous but truthful remark made by the affable Pulitzer-prize-winning ex-newsman and ex-Ambassador from the Philippines, Mr. Carlos Romulo, who once said that at breakfast every morning the section of the Washington newspaper he first turned to was not the sports page, the financial page, or even the comics, but the women's page.

Speaking of cultivation of press contacts, I may add that the embassy press officer would do well to go about this "in a diplomatic way." On the one hand, he must avoid appearing to be too aggressive, pestering the reporters day and night with offers of information or showering them with presents on the slightest pretext, lest this aggressiveness be misconstrued by some as attempts at bribery. On the other hand, he would be remiss if he failed to maintain and nurture the contacts once the initial approach was made.

Occasionally, though, a gem of an idea or a brain wave springs from a chance contact. Let me give you an example. In April of 1966, through the introduction of mutual friends, I met a small number of Congressional summer interns. As you know, Washington is chock full of these young college students from all parts of the United States interning on Capitol Hill. One day, at lunch in a Chinese restaurant, we got to talking about the extent of knowledge on China among American university students in general. "Why don't you invite some of us to the Chinese Embassy for a chat?" one of them, editor of his college paper, suggested casually. Indeed, why not? I talked to the Ambassador, and he liked the idea. The idea grew. After several weeks' planning, an elaborate program of entertainment, music, and folk dancing was prepared, showing the various aspects of Chinese culture. Over 2000 Congressional interns, young Democrats and young Republicans alike, representing virtually all

50 states, came to the Ambassador's reception at Twin Oaks. One of the Washington papers the next day referred to it as a "first" in Embassy Row public relations.

One of our duties as Press Counselor of the Embassy is the handling of press contacts for visiting VIP's from Taiwan, which is no simple matter. Washington, being the most worldly wise of cities, is not too vulnerable to the attractions of foreign visitors, unless he or she is exceptionally famous or ultra-endowed in one form or another. Once we gave a small cocktail party for the press at the National Press Club to meet a VIP from Taipei. Not one line was written in the next day's newspapers. Soon experience forced upon us the conclusion that exclusiveness was perhaps one of the solutions. Before the arrival of the dignitary—a politician, an artist, a musician—we would shop around, so to speak, for a reporter interested in the promise of an exclusive story.

An exception, however, was Madame Chiang Kai-shek, who paid the United States a 14-month visit in 1965-1966, in a private capacity. No stranger to this country, China's First Lady became an immediate attraction the moment the news was flashed from Taipei that she was on her way to America. I had the honor to be designated her press secretary in Washington, which meant that we were in for a hectic 14 months, hectic in the sense that we were kept feverishly active but not restlessly frustrated. We did not have to lift one finger soliciting press contacts. They came to us. Even before Madame arrived in San Francisco, we were already deluged with requests from various mass media—by letter, by telegram, by telephone, and by personal contact—for interviews, for press conferences, for personal appearances, and speaking engagements. How we wished all public relations jobs were that simple!

Our job as press secretary was made so much easier by the magnetic personality of Madame Chiang, whose twin assets of brains and beauty—that rarest combination in any woman anywhere in the world—scored an instant hit everywhere she appeared publicly. She spoke from coast to coast, in the North and in the South. Known widely for her eloquence since her address before a joint session of the U.S. Congress during World War II, her appearances drew vast audiences in the tens of thousands. And tens of millions more saw her on television.

Invitations had come from most of the nation's choicest public forums and television panel shows, including the National Press Club, Washington, D.C.; the Commonwealth Club, San Francisco; the Executive Club, Chicago; the Economic Club, Detroit; The Cosmos Club, Washington D.C.; the World Affairs Council, Los Angeles; the American Association of University Women; the Bull Elephants, Capitol Hill; the National Women's Republic Club; the National Federation of Business and Professional Women; "Meet the Press" and "Issues and Answers"; the United States War College; the U.S. Industrial College of the Armed Forces.

Citing these names, seemingly somewhat monotonous, is intended as an answer to Nationalist China's tiny minority of detractors who claimed that Madame Chiang was "coolly received." How many of the world's women leaders, it may be asked, were offered the platform of that many groups and associations? Furthermore, for every invitation she accepted, she politely declined at least nine or ten others. Had all the invitations been accepted without selection, she probably would have had to speak or make a public appearance two or three times in each of the 61 weeks she spent in this country.

One of the main reasons she was obliged to turn down such a large percentage of invitations was that she simply did not have the time to write that many speeches. As far as I knew, she did not have a ghost-writer in the true sense of the word. Also, she was rather meticulous about literary style and the choice of words, some of which I must say were not too familiar to the average member of the press. She never used the same speech twice, and not once did she even resort to what most speakers practice, merely rearranging what has been said before.

Handling press relations for Madame Chiang was not a burdensome job. Contrary to what was common talk among some press circles, she was not at all fussy, or cantankerous, or impetuous, or demanding. On the contrary, she was courteous, affable, considerate, and generally cooperative toward the press. More than once, although pressed for time when commuting from one function to another while visiting a city or a university, she good-naturedly let herself be ordered around by news photographers not only for "one more" but "one more again." And not once was she rattled by an unfriendly or needling question at any one of her many press conferences.

To be sure, our work involved considerable correspondence and telephone contact before she traveled to any city. Besides the normal routine of preparing advance press notices and mimeographing her speeches, we had to work out her whole schedule with the hosts down to the last minute, from arrival to departure. The most time-consuming part of our work—the hosts were responsible for local publicity—was to contact the various mass media in the neighboring states.

Take, for instance, Madame Chiang's October 20, 1965, "sentimental journey" to Macon, Georgia, her "home town" in America where she had attended Wesleyan College in her teens. We sent personal press notices to 29 newspapers and 16 radio and television stations in Georgia and its neighboring states. We arrived in Macon one day ahead to check over final arrangements for press coverage, in conjunction with the public relations director of the college. It was a satisfying feeling when, shortly after we checked in at the hotel, media reporters' calls started coming in. In addition to front-page stories in several newspapers and live coverage over a number of radio stations on Madame's speech and visit, one of the most rewarding results was a color cover and a five-page illustrated story in the *Atlanta Journal and Constitution* Sunday magazine on Madame's activities.

In the attainment of smooth press arrangements even the most trivial details demand attention. There were, for example, two things about which Madame Chiang was particular. One was that the microphone on the podium, either for a speech or press conference, be neither too high nor too low. We followed this instruction to the letter by always checking and adjusting the microphone to the proper height a few hours before she was to speak so that she did not have to crane her neck or speak at a stooped posture. The second was that under no circumstances should the texts of her speech be distributed until after she finished speaking, the reasoning being that the flipping and rustling of the pages by the reporters would disturb her while she was speaking. To this day Madame Chiang has not been told, but it can be disclosed now that this instruction was never strictly followed. Having myself been a practicing newsman for many years, I knew how important it was for the reporter to have an advance text and have the story written up first. When distributing the advance texts to the press I made the specific request that the moment Madame started speaking, the texts should be in their proper places in the newsmen's pockets and that they refrain from reading or checking them as long as she was speaking. Not once did any member of the press violate this arrangement.

Another of our functions is to promote among the American people an interest in visiting Taiwan. Through tourist literature and documentary films, we show what the real China is like, in contrast to the dismal situation in mainland China, which has in 17 years of communist rule been transformed into an un-Chinese fantasyland and where rampaging Red Guards have been destroying old Chinese culture, old Chinese customs, old Chinese ideology, and old Chinese habits. We are justifiably proud of what we have achieved in Taiwan, from a dislocated economic dependency to an integrated self-sufficiency that has been termed by many objective observers as an economic miracle.

Two great Americans dwelt on this theme in welcoming our Vice President, Mr. C. K. Yen, to the United States recently. "The example of the Republic of China," said President Johnson,

"encourages and inspires us all. Once the economic outlook for Free China was dim indeed. Today an admiring world witnesses these results: since 1952 your per capita gross national product has doubled; since 1960 your exports have tripled; and today you have one of the highest standards of living in Asia. Our sense of common achievement was greatest when, in 1965, I was able to tell the Congress that Free China no longer needed American economic assistance."

In New York, at a dinner in honor of Mr. Yen, Mr. Eugene Black, world-renowned banker, said: "It is no exaggeration to say that Taiwan is an island of great hope in a world whose economic geography is usually described with the statistics of misery."

Because of this immense pride in our progress, we want as many Americans—and other foreign nationals—as possible to see for themselves how efficaciously we have utilized U.S. economic aid in turning Taiwan into what a number of American magazines call "a showplace for the rest of Southeast Asia." In this endeavor we have not been unsuccessful. From January to March 1967 a total of 48,533 foreign visitors came to Taiwan, of whom 603 were from journalistic and academic circles. As this figure showed an increase of 33 percent over that for the corresponding period of 1966, the total for the whole of 1967 was expected to reach a quarter of a million.

Informationally, in this connection there are two services we stand ready to render. First, we maintain a small stock of some 35 documentary films that are available for loan, free of charge, to any groups or organizations. These films depict various aspects of Chinese life—its history, art, industry, tourism, theater, education, crafts, and festivals. Second, we are always more than glad to lend a helping hand, particularly to members of the press, in arranging for visits to Taiwan, such as mapping out a program of sightseeing and interviews, making hotel reservations, and meeting you at the airport if you happen to be without friends over there. This service, however, I hasten to add, should not be confused with what is popularly known as the "officially guided tour" that is required in Communist China. In Taiwan there is absolute freedom of movement and contact for foreign visitors, except of course for certain restricted military areas for security reasons, as common to every country in the world, including the United States. Visitors are free to roam wherever it strikes their fancy, and talk to anyone they please. However, as mentioned earlier, if any newsman should require assistance, we are there to provide it.

A fourth function of the embassy press office is the distribution of the various publications issued by the Government Information Office in Taipei and its contracted services, which are of several varieties. To the first variety belong publications that are issued periodically, such as (a) a daily news bulletin, in both English and Chinese, issued by our New York office; (b) a weekly newspaper, called the *Free China Weekly*, which is edited and published in Taipei and airmailed to the United States; (c) a monthly magazine called the *Free China Review*, which serves a mixed diet of analytical articles on serious national problems as well as human interest features; and (d) a quarterly pictorial called *Vista,* which, largely through photographs and art work, portrays the life, the philosophy, the activities, and the plans and hopes of the Republic of China.

Also available for distribution are two illustrated series. One, under the general title of *China* and the *Chinese Series,* consists of half a dozen folders on Chinese customs, festivals, cooking, music, opera, language, and education. The other is a booklet series of fuller studies on such subjects as land reform, higher education, public health, industrial progress, and China's own technical aid program to Africa.

Because of our limited budget, however, we have to adopt a rather discriminating policy in our distribution of these publications, based on the only sensible principle of maximizing their usefulness. It is calculated that with our small budget we could not afford to send even one postcard to every hundredth person in the United States if we are to treat all the American people indiscriminately as our recipients. We have no intention, therefore, that our publications serve no more useful purpose except to fill wastebaskets. Instead of distributing them on expanded mailing lists supplied by commercial firms, we regard each of our publications, however small or inexpensive, as a gift only to those who ask for it. Thus we assure ourselves that every piece of our literature put in the mails will be read, and read, we hope, with appreciation.

Our fifth function is assigned to us by the popular demand of the American public—to serve as best we can as the walking encyclopedia on China. Requests for information have come to the embassy from all 50 states of the Union, and occasionally from countries beyond America's borders, scattered in all five continents. Sometimes it requires a check at a world atlas before we discover from what corner of the globe the letter began its journey. One new name, for example, figured among letters received while I was writing this chapter, which we would not have known without the aid of the world almanac: Nkonya Ntumda. I am not sure how many of you know the country in which Nkonya Ntumda is situated.

The information the letter-writers seek is extraordinarily far-ranging, from Chinese recipes to Chinese women's headdress in specific ancient dynasties. Most letters from schools and colleges, libraries, and teachers ask for general information on China, such as brochures, pamphlets, maps, posters, etc. Some submit such long questionnaires that if you answered all of them you would be helping them write a term paper. Some solicit our help in locating Chinese friends in Taiwan "who used to study somewhere in the United States." There are others who seek pen pals, ask for Chinese newspapers and magazines as study materials, want the most detailed statistics on various developments in the Republic of China, or suggest the easiest way of our returning to the China mainland.

Even a cursory tabulation indicates that an overwhelming majority of the letters seek explanations on current issues, such as our reasons for thinking Red China unfit for United Nations membership; conditions on the China mainland; the role of native Formosans in the various levels of our government; the views of President Chiang Kai-shek on various issues of international importance; the present and future of Peiping-Moscow relations. We receive an average of 80 letters a day, all of which we strive our utmost to answer as promptly as we can. Except for a few unanswerable queries, very few indeed, all these letter writers are regarded as genuine friends of China who wish only to know us better.

By way of summary, I must say that the case of the Republic of China has proved that image building relies more on the primary ingredients of facts and information rather than on techniques of public relations, although techniques are admittedly important. For in the last analysis, what is done and accomplished in Taiwan has in the long run proved more convincing to the people abroad than what we said, no matter how beautifully and cleverly we said it. As Dr. Daniel Lerner, in his book *Propaganda in War and Crisis,* so perceptively said, one inherent limitation about propaganda is that no matter how shrewdly it is designed and how vigorously it is utilized, it "does not change conditions, but only beliefs about conditions."

This policy of facts more than propaganda serves us well in yet another dimension of our information program. Unlike many other embassies or governments, we are vitally concerned not with just one image—our own—but two. We regard it as an equally important part of our business to put in proper perspective the image of Communist China in the minds of the Americans. We are not referring to the image projected long-distance from Peiping through an endless stream of publications and literature flooding this country, which, unapologetically propagandistic and devoid of objectivity, is generally understood by most Americans to be nothing but propaganda. However, an articulate intellectual segment of America itself, albeit a very small minority, has during the past two decades painted an image of Red China that to us seems to be highly rose-colored, undeservedly over-praised, and its power repetitiously exaggerated. For years it was part of our job to correct such an image by publishing factual reports about the true conditions on the China mainland, but without avail. As late as March 1966, American experts on Communist China were telling the Fulbright Senate Committee what a paradise the Chinese Communists had fashioned for the Chinese people on the mainland, its leadership untouched by any purge since 1949 (something unheard of within the communist bloc), and that the Chinese people by and large were so utterly contented and happy that there was hardly a ripple of dissent or opposition.

Through these years, what we learned—based on information from the underground, intelligence agents, and painstaking study of the mainland press—was exactly the opposite of what the American experts were dishing out. From time to time we issued reports of what actually was happening behind the Bamboo Curtain—rising opposition against the communist regime after the Great Leap Backward, persecution of the intellectuals, infighting within the communist hierarchy, the ousting of Mao Tse-tung by Liu Shao-chi from the presidency in 1959, and so on—only to be labeled by these American experts as "Kuomintang propaganda."

In retrospect, we find with satisfaction that our information program regarding the image of Red China, based on truths and facts, has been vindicated by the current upheavals on the mainland. Many of our reports these last years, however unpopular or how unwelcome at the time, have been proved accurate by the "Great Cultural Revolution," which has at one blow shattered the myth of a stable and monolithic communist regime in power.

13

The Waking Dragon

DR. HAROLD C. HINTON
INSTITUTE FOR SINO-SOVIET STUDIES
GEORGE WASHINGTON UNIVERSITY
WASHINGTON, D.C.

D R. HAROLD C. HINTON, a recognized expert on China and the Far East, is an Associate Professor of International Affairs at George Washington University in Washington, D.C.

Dr. Hinton came by his interest in things international in a very natural fashion. His American parents were in France when he was born in 1924, and he spent his first five years there. From age five to nine, he resided with his parents in Great Britain. He returned to the United States for his education and received his diploma summa cum laude in Classics from St. Paul's School in Concord, New Hampshire, in 1941.

War brought a pause in his education and he was commissioned in the Field Artillery, attended the Infantry School and Military Intelligence Training Center, then served as Military Historian in Okinawa and Korea. He received his AB cum laude in absentia (history) from Harvard in 1946, then took a master's (1948) and PhD (1951) from Harvard in the fields of modern Far Eastern history and politics.

He has taught at Georgetown University, Trinity College, Columbia University, Harvard, and Oxford. He has held numerous fellowships. He has lectured at the National War College, the Inter-American Defense College, the Naval War College, and has appeared as a China expert before the House Subcommittee on the Far East and the Pacific.

His most recent major publication is *Communist China in World Politics* (Houghton Mifflin, 1966).

The Chinese Communist leadership has access to considerable factual information on the outside world, although less in quantity and quality than would be appropriate to a regime striving for great power status. This information, however, is far from being the only ingredient of Chinese policy and propaganda, which are formed to a very great extent out of an underlying Chinese Communist outlook compounded of traditional, modern Chinese, revolutionary Chinese, Marxist-Leninist, and Maoist elements.

In brief, traditional Chinese history contributed to this amalgam a conviction of superiority, especially with respect to the rest of Asia; modern Chinese history contributed a sense of bitterness toward the major powers; the revolutionary period contributed a belief that the Chinese Communist Party, and it alone, has found the organizational techniques and politico-military strategy to unify and modernize China and give it its rightful place in the sun; Marxism-Leninism contributed a sense of belonging to a worldwide and inevitably victorious historic movement in which China can hope to become the leading influence; and the career and "thought" of Mao Tse-tung contributed an ideology and leader around whom Chinese in general can rally, or pretend to rally, so as to escape from their long nightmare of war and chaos in much the same way as the Germans tried to escape by rallying around Adolf Hitler.

Every act of communication by a regime imbued with such an outlook is bound to be an act of propaganda. Propaganda, it will be recalled, has been defined as that branch of the art of lying that consists in almost deceiving one's friends without quite deceiving one's enemies. In the case of Communist China a more accurate description might suggest that the regime has demonstrated an increasing ability to deceive itself combined with a decreasing ability to deceive others.

To some extent this is not an unprecedented trend but reflects an ancient Chinese tendency toward an almost infinite capacity to believe in the truth of one's own nonsense. The effectiveness of this tendency on the Chinese Communist leadership has been enhanced by the fact that before 1949 it had no effective competitor within China, and that since 1949 it has had none at all.

The boundless belief of at least the Maoist segment of the Chinese Communist leadership in the truth and effectiveness of its own propaganda, as contrasted with anyone else's, is shown by its occasional publication of Soviet (but not American) anti-Chinese statements (a courtesy that has not been reciprocated by the Russians), as well as by efforts to smuggle Chinese anti-Soviet propaganda into the Soviet Union and into other Communist-controlled countries.

The kinds of control and pressure that are exerted by systems we call totalitarian can be justified and maintained only in the face of an enemy, real or alleged. In the outlook and propaganda of the Chinese Communists the United States has been Public Enemy Number One since even before 1949. Since 1958 the Soviet Union has been increasingly added to this demonology as a foe perhaps not as dangerous as the United States but even more despicable, because its leaders once knew the truth but have since betrayed it.

There is a tendency in Peking to assume that leaders in the developing countries, to whose Maoist-style revolutionization the Chinese Communists intend to contribute, are in some sense pro-Chinese except for those who are pro-American or pro-Soviet, and conversely to assume that Chinese setbacks in these areas, of which there have been a number in recent years, must be the work of pro-American or pro-Soviet elements, rather than (as is actually the case) the result of Chinese miscalculation of the pace at which proxy revolutions can be usefully forced.

Like any other power, Communist China seeks security from external attack; its anxiety on this score is not diminished by the fact that an impartial observer might conclude that it creates, by its bellicose talk and its occasionally bellicose behavior, most of whatever risks to itself exist. Chinese propaganda constantly asserts that the United States intends to invade or otherwise attack the mainland of China, and that in such a contingency Soviet support cannot be relied on because the Soviet Union is colluding with the United States against China out of its overwhelming fear of American nuclear superiority. Indeed, Chinese propaganda occasionally suggests that Soviet collusion with the United States goes to such lengths that the Soviet Union too might attack China.

In reality the Chinese leadership probably believes that a major armed clash with the United States is "inevitable" in the indefinite future, but that in the near future (a horizon that has a habit of receding as one approaches, so that one never comes to the end of it) this conflict can be avoided or postponed by good management on the part of China. The constant allegations of American aggressive intent, whether fully believed or not by those who make them, seem to have several purposes: to keep the Chinese public in a high state of alertness and loyalty to the regime; to keep world attention focused on American behavior toward China; and to put on the United States the burden of proving that it does not in fact intend to attack China.

In addition, Communist China attempts with some success to employ a hostage strategy against the United States by means of implicit or explicit threats of conventional military retaliation against the mainland Asia, or of future nuclear retaliation against the offshore countries and American bases in them, if the United States actively threatens or actually attacks China. Neutral governments and opinion groups have been wooed by the Chinese, rather skillfully during the Bandung era and more clumsily in recent years, partially in order to exercise political deterrence on the United States through pro-Chinese attitudes in the third world.

The Chinese Communist leadership aspires to influence, and indeed to great power status, on the plane of world affairs, as the leading power in Asia, as the principal energizer of revolution in the developing countries, and as the guiding influence on what remains of the world communist movement. Until recently the Chinese were successful to a degree in the third world and even in the West—where China has been the Shangri La of alienated intellectuals since the eighteenth century—in projecting an image of a regime that had found a path to revolutionary seizure of power and rapid national development unmarred by the corruption, inflation, and excessive coercion that has attended such efforts elsewhere. This image has been badly tarnished, however, by Mao Tse-tung's Great Cultural Revolution, which he has been trying unsuccessfully to internationalize by preaching to all the world the virtues of the "thought of Mao Tse-tung," the Red Guards, and the Little Red Book.

In Orwellian terms, Communist China's Ministry of Truth is the Propaganda Department of the Communist Party's Central Committee, which has remained under firm Maoist control during the Great Cultural Revolution through a series of purges. From the standpoint of foreign propaganda, the most important activity supervised by the department is probably the New China News Agency, which broadcasts extensively in a variety of languages to most regions of the world without benefit of transmitters on foreign soil and maintains offices in a sizable number of countries (noncommunist as well as communist) to disseminate and collect news, or, more accurately, information capable of being developed into propaganda or intelligence.

The principal, although by no means the only, periodical published in Peking for foreign consumption is the *Peking Review,* an attractively produced journal that purveys the purest Maoist line. A stream of books and pamphlets in various languages, some of them containing original material and some only items that have already appeared in the Chinese press, emanates from the Foreign Languages Press.

Other channels through which propaganda is disseminated include Chinese embassies and visiting delegations overseas and occasional clandestine radio stations designed to incite "people's wars" in neighboring countries such as Thailand. Chinese propaganda can be gotten in the United States, by parties interested for scholarly or other reasons, in a variety of ways. Radio Peking can be received on shortwave radio sets. Printed propaganda can be ordered through distributors in Hong Kong or the United States. There are two authorized distributors of Communist Chinese materials in the United States, one in New York and one in San Francisco, who deposit sums credited to Peking in special blocked accounts, the contents of which Peking may or may not ever see.

It seems probable that the Chinese leadership would like, as its technological capabilities progress, to have communications satellites of its own, or failing that to use the satellites of other countries. The thought of Chinese propaganda, already rather obtrusive, being made more or less omnipresent in this way is a sobering one.

The content of Communist Chinese propaganda is strongly characterized by onesidedness, oversimplification, suppression, exaggeration, repetition, and the use of largely meaningless slogans to create in the mind of the perceiver an overwhelming if perhaps vague general impression of the total rightness of the Chinese point of view. The actual effect, of course, varies according to the mentality of the person in question. The following passage from an issue (April 7, 1967) of the *Peking Review,* taken literally at random from the shelf, conveys the point.

Under the personal leadership of the great teacher, great leader, great supreme commander and great helmsman Chairman Mao, China's great proletarian cultural revolution, the broadest, most profound and largest revolutionary mass movement in world history, is entering a new stage of winning decisive victory.

China's proletarian revolutionaries are closing their ranks and, forming an irresistible torrent of the great proletarian cultural revolution, are launching a fierce general offensive against a handful of persons in the Party who are in authority and taking the capitalist road: they are carrying out the struggle for the seizure of power. The revolutionary people of the whole world are encouraged and inspired by the excellent situation in China which is seething with enthusiasm.

This sort of thing cries out for parody; in one case known to the writer, someone succeeded in inserting copies of a pirated and uproariously parodied version of another Chinese foreign language propaganda periodical into the regular distribution channels. From the fact that copies of this masterpiece are hard to come by, I gather that it is a collector's item greatly treasured by its fortunate recipients.

Apart from a few positive themes, such as (formerly) the Five

Principles of Peaceful Coexistence and the alleged traditional friendship between China and the country in question (say, Sark-han), and currently the Great Cultural Revolution and its even greater Helmsman, the negative themes of Chinese propaganda have grown increasingly obtrusive. The main one perhaps is that of the necessity for, and the alleged fact of, struggle and revolution against American "imperialism" throughout the world (the "rural areas of the world" against the "cities of the world").

In leftist circles Chinese propaganda stresses about equally strongly the need for struggle against Soviet "revisionism" and all its manifestations. Probably the main single effort is the one to isolate the developing countries from the United States and the Soviet Union, intrinsically a difficult operation in view of the importance of American and Soviet economic aid. The Chinese make extensive use of Afro-Asian unofficial leftist front organizations for this purpose, and would also have used the governmental Afro-Asian Conference that was to have convened at Algiers in 1965 if it had not been torpedoed largely by China's insistence on having its own way and, in particular, on excluding the Soviet Union.

The medium is *not* the message, much less the massage. The impressive energy and technical skill displayed by the Chinese Communists in their propaganda effort, as well as in other activities, has been to a large extent canceled out by political blunders at home and abroad. Communist China's objectives are too grandiose and its methods too obtrusive, in Asia at any rate. The influence of Mao Tse-tung, although emotionally exciting or at least confusing, is intellectually stultifying. The Great Cultural Revolution, presumably his last hurrah, stands little chance of ultimate success in China and even less of spreading abroad. In particular areas, such as the Arab world (Nasser) and Latin America (Castro), the Chinese have little chance of competing successfully for influence with indigenous leaders and would-be regional messiahs.

It is possible, of course, that with the passing of Mao his successors may settle for a policy and a propaganda less grandiose and therefore more effective over the long run. In the meantime, however, recall what Bismarck said of Italy: What a pity that it has such a large appetite and such poor teeth.

14

The Press and
the Public

SHUN-ICHI YAMANAKA
INFORMATION COUNSELOR
EMBASSY OF JAPAN

SHUN-ICHI YAMANAKA is a career diplomat. Born in Osaka in 1918, he passed his Higher Foreign Service exams in 1942 and graduated from Osaka University of Commerce in 1943.

His first foreign post was with the Embassy of Japan in Washington, D.C., to which he came in 1951 as a Third Secretary. He was transferred to the embassy in Buenos Aires in 1952. In 1957 he was named Program Officer to the United Nations Secretariat's Economic Commission for Asia and the Far East in Bangkok. A year later, he was named Program Officer to the United Nations Secretariat's Bureau of Technical Assistance Operations in New York.

He returned to the Ministry of Foreign Affairs in 1961 as Chief of the Economic and Social Section, United Nations Bureau, in Tokyo. In 1963 he was named Chief of the Security Section for North American Affairs in Tokyo.

With his wife and three children, he returned to Washington in 1965 as Counselor to the Embassy of Japan.

IN SPITE of the fact that the United States was mainly responsible for opening up Japan to the Western world in the 1850's, before World War II the general American public had only the haziest idea about Japan and the Japanese.

Fujiyama, geishas, cherry blossoms, and rickshaws pulled by little brown men in straw coolie-hats—this was about the sum total of knowledge of Japan possessed by most Americans. The war, of course, changed all that, and for the worse. Japanese were now thought of as treacherous, buck-teethed sadists, for all practical purposes subhuman.

The Allied Occupation, by giving thousands and thousands of American officers and men the opportunity to rediscover for themselves that the Japanese were human, after all, and possessed of many social and cultural values not normally evident on the field of battle, was instrumental in rebuilding the shattered image of the Japanese as a civilized people.

The main aim, then, of Japanese information activities in the United States after the Peace Treaty has been patiently to build up, in the American public's mind, the true picture of the new Japan: a Japan that has, in its Constitution, forever renounced war as a sovereign right of the nation and the threat or use of force as means of settling international disputes; a Japan whose people are now irrevocably committed to the Western free world and the democratic way of life; a Japan with a highly educated, hard-working population overcoming severe hardships in order to raise not only their own living standard, but also, through trade and aid, that of the less fortunate members of the Asian community; in short, a trustworthy ally capable of and entitled to complete equality in its relations with the United States.

159

Before discussing Japan's information activities in the United States, I would like to give you, by way of background, a description of the state of the press in Japan today.

In a land area comparable to the single state of California, one-twentieth the size of the United States, Japan has a population of over 98 million people, 99.6 percent literate. Because most of the major population and industrial centers of the country are concentrated in a narrow coastal strip starting from the Tokyo-Yokohama complex, running through Osaka-Kobe on the Inland Sea, and ending 540 miles southwest at the Kita-Kyushu complex, conditions are more suitable for a few giant national newspapers than for a host of small local papers.

In 1965, according to statistics compiled in 1966 by the Japan Newspaper Publishers and Editors Association, there were 114 daily newspapers in Japan with a combined circulation of more than 29,777,000. In Japan, besides the usual morning and evening newspapers found throughout the world, there are what are known as "set" papers. Persons subscribing to "set" papers pay one subscription fee, but receive both a morning and an evening paper. The circulation of Japanese newspapers, therefore, differs according to whether "set" papers are counted as one or two. When counted as one, the total circulation of daily newspapers in Japan as of October 1965 was 29,777,000 and when counted as two, 44,135,000.

The *Asahi,* the *Yomiuri,* and the *Mainichi* are the three largest newspapers in Japan; in fact, they are the three largest newspapers in the world, in circulation. In March 1967 the *Asahi* published 5,150,000 copies of its morning edition and 3,390,000 copies of its evening edition. By way of comparison, and implying no disparagement, the circulation of the *New York Times* is around 652,000 for weekdays and 1,355,000 for Sundays. The figures I have just mentioned for the *Asahi* are for every day of the week, 362 days of the year, because Japanese newspapers have only three holidays a year: New Year's Day; May 5, the day of the Boys' Festival; and September 23, the day of the Autumn Equinox.

Today there is complete freedom of the press in Japan, and there is no censorship of any kind. Before and during the war there was a military censorship, and during the occupation the Occupation Authorities exercised a certain amount of control, but after the end of occupation, with the signing of the Peace Treaty in 1951, the Japanese press has been completely free. It is well to remember this, because outside the major powers of the Western free world, this is a rare phenomenon indeed.

The Japan Newspaper Publishers and Editors Association is an organization whose basic purpose is to raise the ethical levels of Japanese newspapers, and in 1946, it drafted and adopted a "Canons of Journalism" as a basic guide in ensuring the freedom, the impartiality, the responsibility, and the dignity of news reports and commentaries. All members of the association, regardless of their size, have pledged to abide by the Canons of Journalism and to regulate their activities and operations in keeping with democratic ideals.

The members of the Japanese press, whether editors, reporters, or cameramen, are a tremendously aggressive breed. Any VIP foreign visitor to Japan usually undergoes his baptism of Japanese press coverage right at the airport, with a heavy barrage of flashbulbs.

In order to regulate the intense competition the Diet, the Prime Minister's office, and all the major ministries of the Government are covered by their own "Press Clubs," to which any newsman wishing to gather news originating from that particular agency has to belong.

For instance, as of April 1967, 14 newspapers and other press agencies (including television news sections) had a total of 110 men covering the Ministry of Foreign Affairs as members of what is known as the "Kasumi Club," "Kasumi" being an abbreviation of "Kasumigaseki," which can be translated as "The Barrier of Mists," a place-name corresponding to the American "Foggy Bottom."

In the Kasumi Club the big three had a total of 37 men, the *Asahi* 12, the *Mainichi* 15, and the *Yomiuri* 10. Each reporter has his specialty, political, economic, cultural, and so forth, and the captain or "Cap" of each team, usually the man with the greatest experience and seniority in the club for that particular paper, deals out such special assignments to each member of the team as the daily situation may require. That is, he indicates what stories are likely to break, what sources the team members should approach, etc.

All club members are expected to get to know key personnel in the Ministry, and as Japan has nothing corresponding to an Official Secrets Act they are free to circulate through the various offices at will.

The Public Information Bureau of the Ministry arranges the official press conferences, interviews, and briefing sessions for the members of the club whenever events require, and also holds similar sessions for members of the foreign press.

As may be imagined, such a "closed" system of newsgathering, although originally designed to eliminate excessive competition within the Japanese press community itself, has led to some criticism from foreign press correspondents. As of December 1966, The Foreign Correspondents Club of Japan had a total of 151 organizations, 306 members.

The Japanese clubs' reply to such criticism is that they are not exclusive at all, but because only a limited number of foreign correspondents are sufficiently proficient in the Japanese language to avail themselves of the various facilities offered to club members in the Japanese language, and because no foreign news agency has sufficient staff to belong to all the clubs simultaneously, the method of newsgathering for the foreign correspondents has of necessity to be different. As mentioned previously, however, the Ministry of Foreign Affairs is cognizant of the problem, and is doing its best to facilitate the reporting of foreign correspondents.

It would appear from such outstanding Tokyo dispatches as those of Robert O. Trumbull of the *New York Times,* Richard Halloran of the *Washington Post,* and others, that the foreign correspondents in Japan are doing excellent jobs in spite of the handicaps.

One further illustration concerning the fierce competition in the Japanese press community: There is a custom known as "Yo-uchi asa-gake," which can perhaps be translated as "attacks under cover of night and before the dawn." Anyone who may have important information on impending or unfolding events is likely to receive a visit at home from one or more reporters late at night or early in the morning. Because the reporters have sedulously cultivated the "contact" for just such an emergency, and are in most cases well known by the unfortunate recipient of such a call, the duties of the host make it mandatory to provide at least a round of drinks—the reporter or reporters and the host eventually engaging in a battle of capacities, with the prize being possession of the cat in the bag.

I could go on to say something about the technical equipment and plant of the Japanese newspapers, which in many cases is the most advanced in the world, not even excepting the United States, but as this is not particularly essential to the present discussion I should just like to mention, in passing, that the caliber of the members of the Japanese press community has never been higher; most of them are university graduates, hired only after passing intensely competitive exams, both written and oral. For most of the major newspapers the rate of competition for the selective exams is in the vicinity of 20 to one. The social position of the members of the press has risen accordingly, although as marital prospects they still suffer somewhat from the irregularity of their hours.

At this point I should like to add a few words about the mass communication media other than the newspapers. In 1966 the total number of television sets in use in Japan was estimated to be around 20 million. As Japan has around 24 million households, the dissemination rate of television is around 75 percent—second only to the United States. The number of standard-wave radio sets is estimated at roughly 30 million sets, or an average of 1.4 to a family, and the number of FM radio sets is estimated at 4 million, or a dissemination rate of 15 to 17 percent of the total households in Japan.

The public-owned national broadcasting network, the Japan Broadcasting Corporation, which would be roughly comparable to the British BBC, operates two separate national radio networks, two separate national television networks, and one national experimental FM radio network. As of February 1966 there were 168 standard-wave radio stations in its First Network, 129 standard-wave radio stations in its Second Network, 373 stations in its General Television Network, 364 stations in its Educational Television Network, and 62 stations in its experimental FM radio network, which also transmits experimental stereophonic broadcasts.

There are 59 commercial broadcasting companies in Japan, of which 13 are radio broadcasting companies only, including one shortwave station. Another 13 are television broadcasting companies only, whereas 33 companies broadcast both radio and television. These commercial broadcasting companies operate a total of 142 standard-wave radio stations, two shortwave stations, and 334 television stations.

In the United States a Japanese reader is overwhelmed by the amount of advertising in the daily papers. One literally has to "search" for the news. In Japanese papers, which have fewer pages than their American counterparts to begin with, a survey made in November 1965 showed the following composition of newspaper pages.

Editorials	1.1	percent
Foreign news	3.5	percent
Political news	6.5	percent
Economic news	8.5	percent
City news	13.3	percent
Culture	14.8	percent
Sports news	8.4	percent
Fiction	2.0	percent
Others	4.2	percent
Total news	62.3	percent
Advertising	37.7	percent
Average number of pages per day	20.4	

It is interesting to note that the majority of the Japanese people recognize the social function of advertising in the present economic life of the nation, with 73.0 percent of those interviewed in a recent survey showing a reaction of acceptance and 9.6 percent a reaction of nonacceptance. However, the Japanese people in general are critical of advertising, with 53.1 percent having had bad impressions of advertising and only 27.1 percent favorable impressions.

The reaction of the Japanese people toward advertising, according to media, is as follows.

	favorable	unfavorable
Newspaper advertising	59.0 percent	10.1 percent
Radio commercials	26.4 percent	30.9 percent
Television commercials	27.5 percent	44.9 percent

Television commercials are obviously as heartily disliked in Japan as in the United States, which augurs well for the further growth of mutual understanding between our two peoples.

The same survey revealed that the Japanese people expect newspapers to be a record of news events and a source of detailed reports. They look forward to television for its entertainment and explanatory qualities. Radios are regarded as a source for bulletin news. Newspapers are "useful," "unpretentious," and "dispassionate." Radios conjure up an image of "speed." Television, on the other hand, is "interesting," "colorful," and "intense."

I shall now turn to Japanese information activities in the United States, and, in particular, to the role of our embassy in this field.

Besides the Embassy of Japan in Washington, D.C., and the Permanent Delegation to the United Nations in New York, Japan has nine consulates-general in the United States: in New York, Chicago, New Orleans, Houston, Seattle, Portland, San Francisco, Los Angeles, and Honolulu. Some of these establishments have only three or four officers from Tokyo, not nearly sufficient to carry out intensive information activities. Therefore, although each consulate-general has at least one officer who handles information matters among his other duties, the bulk of our information effort in the United States, from the viewpoint of both staff and funds, has been entrusted to our Information Center in New York, a part of the consulate-general there.

Japan has information or cultural centers located in 10 embassies and three consulates-general in 13 countries; this year, we plan to open two more, one at the embassy in Mexico and one at our consulate-general in Hong Kong. To many Americans it seems strange that we should have our information services in New York instead of at the embassy in Washington, and the embassy has to send quite a number of inquiries and requests for information it receives to New York for processing.

The basic item of printed material on Japan that we provide on request is a 100-odd page booklet entitled *The Japan of Today,* giving a brief summary of the geography, history, government, economy, social problems, and cultural life of the country, with appropriate color photographs. This booklet and condensations of the booklet for mass distribution to schools are now printed in English, Russian, French, Spanish, German, Chinese, Italian, Portuguese, Swedish, Danish, Finnish, Rumanian, Burmese, Thai, Indonesian (Malay), and Swahili.

We also have a series of separate "Fact Sheets" on different subjects, condensing information on various subjects such as flower arrangement, the tea ceremony, Kabuki, Japanese literature, Japanese music, the economy of Japan, the government of Japan, and so forth, in convenient form for mass distribution to interested groups.

Some 30 to 40 16 mm color films on various Japanese subjects are also available for free rental to the public through a film rental library commissioned by the Japanese Consulate-General in New York and many of the items are also available at our embassy here and the consulates-general throughout the country.

Naturally, the Ambassador, the Consuls-General, and many staff members are in constant demand for speeches, addresses, and participation in seminars and discussions, and all efforts are made to provide a speaker or a participant who is knowledgeable in the field to be covered. Whenever there is a fair-sized audience this kind of direct contact is always highly desirable.

All sorts of inquiries pour in, at the rate of 20 to 30 a day for each establishment. Some are simple requests that can be answered by sending out printed material with a complimentary slip, but some are terribly time consuming, taking a considerable amount of work on the part of the hard-pressed staff to dig up the answers. There is also the usual admixture of crackpot letters that turn up in any country and that we usually ignore.

The embassy must also be prepared to assist the Japanese correspondents in Washington. The Japanese press, as of March 1966, and according to data provided by the Japan Newspaper Publishers and Editors Association, had 262 correspondents stationed abroad, of whom 76 were in the United States (26 in

Washington, 24 in New York, 10 in Los Angeles, and eight each in San Francisco and Honolulu).

The Japanese correspondents in Washington, who form the largest foreign correspondents corps in the capital, larger even than the British, of course all speak English and have no trouble gathering news on their own. The Ambassador holds a general background briefing session every two months, and whenever he meets with someone of importance in the U.S. Government there is a special press conference.

The embassy also holds general background briefing sessions for members of the American press and the wire agencies, and tries to set up press conferences for visiting VIP's from Japan.

With the great speedup in communications, and the preference of all governments to make major policy announcements in their own capitals, it is very seldom that the embassy is called on to break important news here in Washington. From time to time there may be occasions for simultaneous releases in Tokyo and Washington, but on such occasions the releasing agency here in Washington is either the White House or the State Department, and the embassy is only involved in coordinating the date and the time. Because there is a 13- or 14-hour difference in time between Tokyo and Washington, arranging a time suitable to both capitals can sometimes be quite a headache—especially when morning edition and evening edition deadlines have to be taken into account.

I should like to take this opportunity to mention that the Japanese Ministry of Foreign Affairs also has a program to invite foreign editors and newspapermen to Japan to take a firsthand look at conditions in Japan. Although funds are limited, we managed to invite a total of 35 members of the press to Japan between April 1966 and March 1967, for periods ranging from three to 16 days. The geographical representation of the invitees was eight from Asia, one from Oceania, one from North America (a reporter from the Canadian paper *Toronto Globe and Mail*), five from Central and South America, eight from Western Europe, 11 from the Middle East, and one from Africa.

A most noteworthy recent development, from the viewpoint of news communications between the United States and Japan, was the start of international telecommunications relay via satellite and its epochal impact on television and newspapers. In April 1965 a commercial communications satellite, the Intelsat I, sometimes referred to as the Early Bird, was placed over the Atlantic Ocean to link Europe and the United States by both telecommunications and television relay. In January and March 1967 two Intelsat II satellites were successfully orbited, one over the Pacific and one over the Atlantic, launching epoch-making television transmissions linking Japan and the United States, the United States and Europe.

During 1968 a third series of three commercial communications satellites was scheduled to be launched over the Pacific, the Atlantic, and the Indian oceans, which, with the earlier satellites, would complete the global network for telecommunications via satellite relays.

This is expected to have an incalculable effect on not only the television industry but also on newspaper coverage of international events.

Finally, the relations between the Japanese and the foreign newspaper worlds have grown closer with each passing year. The year 1966 saw Japan's relations, particularly with the press of various Asian countries, greatly strengthened. The Japan Newspaper Publishers and Editors Association in October 1965 launched a program of technical aid to Asian newspapers, with the cooperation of the Asian Secretariat of the International Press Institute.

This Asian Aid Program has continued to expand, and in August 1966 the Japan Newspaper Publishers and Editors Association held its second seminar on printing techniques. This was followed in October by a seminar on photographic techniques attended by trainees from various countries. In November a Japan–Republic of Korea Editorial Seminar was held in Tokyo, attended by newspaper executives of influential Korean newspapers. The seminar was a great success.

In addition, newspapermen from various Asian countries and a large number of newsmen from Europe and the United States visited Japan in 1966 to study newspaper conditions in Japan. International exchanges in both the editorial and technical fields are expected to continue to expand in the coming years.

It is our hope that the press and other mass communications media of both our countries will continue to maintain their steady and healthy growth. A well-informed and knowledgeable public, aware not only of national affairs but also of developments in the outside world, continues to be the best guarantee for world peace. Many experts believe that not poverty but ignorance is the main factor retarding the progress of so many of the developing nations today. Our countries, which are happy in possessing a vigorous and responsible press, should not be content to sit back and rest on our achievements, but should join hands in a common effort to bring about a similar happy state of affairs on a global basis. For, after all, as Barbara Ward mentions in her *Spaceship Earth,* we share not only a rapidly shrinking world, but also a common destiny.

15

Jujitsu Public Relations

PO SUNG KIM
INFORMATION ATTACHÉ
EMBASSY OF KOREA

P̲ᴏ ꜱᴜɴɢ ᴋɪᴍ, director of the Korean Information Office in Washington, D.C., was born in Seoul in 1929. He graduated from Yonsei University, a Presbyterian Mission School in Seoul.

Mr. Kim worked as a correspondent for Reuters from 1950 to 1961, with assignments in Seoul, Tokyo, Singapore, London, Hong Kong, and New York. During this period he studied at Northwestern University in the United States on a brief leave of absence from Reuters.

Mrs. Kim, who resides in Virginia with Mr. Kim and their two children, worked for the Overseas Branch of the Korean Broadcasting System as an English-language announcer for the last six years of Mr. Kim's Reuters employment. She also attended Yonsei University.

In 1961 Mr. Kim came to Washington to serve the Korean government. Since then he has been a member of the presidential party during the state visit of President Chung Hee Park to the United States in May 1965; Press Officer in the Korean delegation to the Manila Summit Conference in October 1966; and Press Officer for the Korean government during President Johnson's state visit to Korea in November 1966.

Ever since four sailors from a New Bedford whaler, the *Two Brothers,* landed on the eastern coast of Korea on July 1, 1855, goodwill and friendship have bound the United States and the "Land of Morning Calm" in the Asian peninsula.

As a representative of the Korean government engaged in a public relations program in the United States, I have the honor of presenting an outline of our activities.

The most important purpose is reaffirmation of the traditional friendship and goodwill existing between the two nations. The United States, in concluding the formal diplomatic treaty with the then "Hermit Kingdom" of Korea on May 22, 1882, recognized Korea's true independence and became the first Western power to recognize Korea's sovereignty—much to the displeasure of China.

Korea also wishes to make the American public aware of her appreciation of American assistance: the missionaries and teachers who introduced Western civilization to Korea; the servicemen who, in snow-covered hills and muddy trenches, defended Korea in 1950–1953; the economic assistance that enabled our country to recover from the ravages of war; and all those individuals and groups—too numerous to mention—who aided Korea in her time of trouble.

Korea wishes to inform the United States of her efforts toward economic self-sufficiency, democratic political development, and collective security in Asia and the world. Korea wants to tell the stories of her diplomatic achievements, her gallant forces fighting side by side with the American soldiers in the jungles of Vietnam, her industrial climate, which has presented the world with the most favorable investment conditions, and her culture, which presents visitors with one of the most sophisticated and romantic ancient civilizations of the world.

Most important of all, Korea wants to let the American public know that our two nations are bound forever by trust, their opposition to communism, and a firm determination to remain free.

Guiding principles of the Korean government information program are honesty, sincerity, and frugality. The entire program is geared to tell the true story of Korea, her people, culture, and government. No attempt is made to engage in propaganda for any administration or any single leader. Mistakes, if any, are explained but never covered up. Because the country is not yet "wealthy," common sense and frugality are strictly observed. Rather than hire costly professionals in the public relations field, we depend on the personal efforts of our staff members.

Korea works against very stiff competition in the field of public relations in the United States. More than 110 nations maintain information offices and staffs in the Washington–New York area alone. Korea is relatively new in this field, as the country only became independent in 1948.

Currently, the information activity is endeavoring to introduce a long-range policy to compete against other nations, and sometimes to work together to seek "wider impact" of the information program. With limited resources, the personal efforts of the staff are doubly important.

Talks to private groups, meetings, and lectures to university and college classes on international affairs are usually more effective, and certainly much cheaper, than expensive publications and audiovisual materials.

Whenever possible, "yudo (Korean word for jujitsu) public relations" is employed. Under this policy, an airline or steamship company serving Korea gladly cooperates with her in its own public relations program. Many publications accept articles on Korea written by Koreans. Trade publications of firms with investment in or business relations with Korea are important public relations media. "Letters to the Editor" columns of newspapers and magazines are important areas in which Korea can express her viewpoint. There are other means of utilizing available resources for public relations for Korea at little or no financial cost to the country.

One or two hours of sincere conversation with an influential writer may bring about an article that—in terms of space—may be worth several thousand dollars if purchased as an advertisement.

No information activity can be handled adequately by an office with only three staff members, so Korea is fortunate in having vast "human resources" to call on, and to receive much friendly and sympathetic cooperation.

There are about 2,500,000 Americans—a great many of whom now hold important civilian positions—who fought in Korea in 1950–1953 and have served in Korea in the postwar years. These servicemen have what I may call sentimental investments in Korea. Their concern about Korea's progress helps to keep alive the general American interest in Korea.

American churches and schools have maintained missionaries and teachers in Korea since 1883, apart from a brief interruption in 1940–1945. Most of them have now retired, but their voice is still very influential.

A small number of American newspapermen did visit Korea before 1945, but since the outbreak of the war in Korea in 1950 hundreds of American newspaper and radio commentators have reported on Korea. Thus, scattered throughout the United States, there are people in senior editorial positions who have a profound insight into Korean affairs.

Korea has about 18,000 residents and students in the United States, and they are—without exception—Korea's cultural ambassadors. Although their political views may differ to some degree, their attachment to the motherland is strong and they are an important means of cultural and informational exchange between the two countries.

There are 22 churches and several centers serving Koreans in the United States, and Koreans operate dozens of stores and restaurants, publish newspapers and periodicals, and sponsor many functions such as "Korea Nights."

There are more than 150 Korean professors and associate professors in American universities and colleges. Hundreds of doctors, dentists, and medical technicians work in American medical centers. Most of them are indeed the cream of the Korean society, and they have a relatively high standing among minority groups in the United States.

Korea maintains an embassy in Washington, a mission at the United Nations, consulates-general in Hawaii, New York, Los Angeles, and San Francisco, and an honorary consul in Chicago. Korea also has trade missions in several major cities in the United States. Tourist associations maintain branches in New York and other major cities. Private Korean business firms operate their own U.S. offices. All these government and business offices cooperate with the Korean Information Office in Washington, D.C., in public relations activities.

As this is written there are 23 goodwill organizations in the United States that have a direct bearing on all promotion of friendship and culture between the two countries. Beside these, which are more or less exclusively concerned with the United States and Korea, 85 religious and social agencies and foundations belong to the Korean Association of Voluntary Agencies. These organizations also sponsor tours of cultural groups such as the Little Angels and the Korean Children's Choir.

Five American cities have established "sisterhood" ties with Korean cities.

At least 60 American scholars are currently engaged in research on Korean affairs. Ten universities in the United States offer Korean language courses. Major museums and research centers have at least one staff member who follows Korean affairs.

Several universities such as Long Island and Western Michigan have conducted symposiums on Korean studies.

Until 1962 Korea was not really on the tourist map, but in 1966 60,000 tourists came to Korea and of this number about 65 percent were Americans. Upon their return to the United States they often show slides and films of Korea to groups of friends.

Since 1953 an average of 700 American servicemen a year have married Korean girls. Back in the United States this led to the formation of the American-Korean Wives Club, and the Washington chapter has 100 members.

Koreans operate radio programs in Hawaii and Los Angeles and they publish about 12 weekly or monthly publications. Some

American periodicals such as *The Asian Student, The Asian Survey,* and *The Far Eastern Quarterly* regularly report Korean affairs.

The Korean Information Office in Washington, D.C., publishes a 32-page quarterly called *Korean Report.* This magazine, with a worldwide circulation of 33,000, is one of the major publications of the foreign governments in the United States and is aimed at readership level above that of the high-school student.

For general information a 24-page booklet entitled *Guide to Korea* is provided. This is revised and brought up to date several times a year, and about 100,000 copies are printed each year.

For Korean students and residents in the United States a 24-page biweekly magazine, *News From Korea,* is printed in Korea and distributed by the Korean Information Office. About 3000 copies of this Korean-language publication are being distributed in the United States.

The Ministry of Public Information in Seoul—plus other government departments, tourist and business associations—also provides the Korean Information Office with a number of books and periodicals. Some of the most sought-after publications are: *Information Series, Korea Today, Korea Seen From Abroad, New Aspects of Korea, Korea Photo News,* and *Democratic Republican Party Bulletins.*

The Ministry of Public Information is Seoul also provides the KIO with motion picture films, color slides, musical records, exhibit materials, posters, calendars, paintings, flags, costumes, and photographs for exhibitions in the United States.

In return the ministry receives reference and information material from the United States through the Korean Information Office. This helps the government to formulate its over-all overseas information program.

The Korean Information Office also handles inquiries and an average of 200 letters and 40 telephone calls each day. It maintains a library for the benefit of students, professors, and newspapermen.

The Information Office staff sponsor and/or assist with "Korea Nights," fashion shows, bazaars, movie showings, and lectures. The wives of staff members are also active in the women's events in the Washington area.

The Ministry of Public Information in Seoul maintains four overseas information offices: Tokyo, Washington, Paris, and Saigon. In addition, an official is attached to the Consul General in Osaka. The KIO in Washington covers the entire Western Hemisphere from Canada to Brazil.

The Korean government does not employ professional agencies, nor does it have any American staff or lobbyists.

There are some factors that are disadvantageous to Korea. For example, Korea is still a relatively poor country with a per capita income of $123. This, coupled with the size of the country (Korea is no bigger than Indiana) means that Korea does not present a very attractive "front."

Other disadvantageous factors are the following:

· Korea's importance in world affairs has not been spectacular. Recent achievements and participation in world diplomacies have yet to be told.

· Like other developing Asian countries that were under dominent Confucianism, Korea was left out of the modern industrial revolution and accordingly lost her chance to contribute to the development of modern technology and industrialization. No Korean has won a Nobel Prize.

· Korea lacks so-called strategic resources—oil, gas, and radioactive materials.

· History has been unkind in the sense of presenting her with so-called world-famous uniqueness. Koreans invented one of the most scientific alphabets, the world's first iron-clad warship, the first movable type, the first encyclopedia, and one of the world's oldest space observation techniques, but the great powers of the world developed atomic energy, aircraft, and rockets, which, in the twentieth century, overshadow Korea's contribution to world civilization.

· The impression of the Korean war dies hard for a substantial majority of Americans. Korea has scarcely lost its reputation as a cold, barren, and economically bleak country. Clashes at the Korean frontier still occur—15 years after the armistice—and such incidents erroneously present an impression of instability along the border.

· Geographically, because it is located amid great powers

(Russia, China, and Japan), few scholars venture to study Korea as a specialty. Korea is frequently included merely as a supplementary subject in the study of Asia.

· In public relations activities in the United States, being an Asian nation poses distinct disadvantages compared to major European nations. The Korean minority in the United States is still very small, so that for most Americans Korea does not spring readily to mind as a place to read about or visit.

· Two revolutions, one in 1960 and the other in 1961, gave an impression to the general American public of a certain lack of political maturity; and although there has been a spectacular development in political and economic sectors since the last revolution, certain areas of enlightenment still remain.

· In recent years American interests in Korea have shown a marked increase. Still, only 42 books on Korea have been published in the United States in the last five years, whereas in 1965 120 books on China alone were published.

· Differences between Korea and the United States in historical background, culture, religion, and customs are all factors that make it difficult for an information staff to win easy and wide understanding.

· Although substantially reduced, Korea still receives a limited amount of economic aid and military support from the United States. This "reliance" on the United States discourages Korea from sponsoring costly and gala promotional activities.

· Last, but not least, is the general "unknownness" of Korea among the general public. It was only in 1950 that Korea became a common word to the United States.

On the plus side of the ledger, there are six important factors that are decidedly advantageous to Korea.

· National interest of the United States and Korea has remained unconflicting throughout history.

· Korea remains strongly pro-American, and Korea is unique in the world in the sense that there has never been an anti-American demonstration.

· America has a vast commitment in Korea, morally to defend her freedom, and financially in the nearly 4 billion dollars that have been contributed. During the Korean war 33,000 American servicemen gave their lives and 140,000 suffered battle injuries. Korea's political and intellectual maturity is raising her position in Asia as one of the most hopeful nations.

· Steady growth in all aspects in Korea has caused it to be termed a source of pride to Americans and made Korea a proud showcase of mutual cooperation.

· Korea and the United States face no disagreements or disputes in their relationships.

· Korea's normalization of relations with Japan, her leading role in Asian and Pacific cooperation, and her participation in the war in Vietnam are greeted by the Americans with a deep sense of appreciation and welcome.

These advantageous factors generally outweigh the so-called disadvantageous factors. Achievements of Korea's government and general development in Korea have made Korean informational activities in the United States easier and the rewards more fruitful.

16

United Nations: A Rich Source of Information

MARCIAL TAMAYO
DIRECTOR
UNITED NATIONS INFORMATION CENTRE
WASHINGTON, D.C.

MARCIAL TAMAYO is a national of Bolivia, born in La Paz and educated in Bolivia and Argentina. He entered the Bolivian diplomatic service in 1944 and was assigned to the Bolivian Embassy in Buenos Aires in 1945. In 1948 he was appointed a Permanent Representative of Bolivia to the United Nations, a post he held until joining the United Nations Secretariat in 1961. During the first eight years of this period, he was also active in research and teaching at the University of La Paz. In 1956 he left his university teaching post to become Press Secretary to the President of Bolivia.

Mr. Tamayo's contact with the United Nations was close. He was his country's representative to the twelfth session of the General Assembly and he was Chairman of the Bolivian Delegation to the thirteenth General Assembly. During the fourteenth General Assembly he was elected to chair the Second (Economic and Financial) Committee. In 1961 the contact became complete and he was appointed Director of the United Nations Information Centre in Rio de Janeiro. He held this post until his transfer to Washington, D.C., as Director of the United Nations Information Centre in that city.

THE purpose, mandate, and activities of the information arm of an intergovernmental organization are different from those of a national information service.

Since 1946 the functions of the United Nations Office of Public Information have been discussed periodically by the General Assembly, and in a series of resolutions the assembly has sought to define the principles under which OPI should conduct its activities.

The principles adopted by the assembly concerning the public information activities of the United Nations may be summarized as follows.

· The basic policy of the United Nations, in the field of public information, is to promote to the greatest extent possible an informed public understanding of the work and purposes of the organization among the peoples of the world.

· To this end, the Department of Public Information should primarily assist and rely on the services of existing official and private agencies of information, educational institutions, and nongovernmental organizations.

· The United Nations Department of Public Information should not engage in propaganda.

· It should undertake, on its own initiative, positive informational efforts to supplement the services of existing agencies.

· It should give priority to the needs of regions in which information media are less well developed.

In order to carry out the public information activities as delineated by the General Assembly the Office of Public Information has been organized functionally as follows: Press and

Publications Division, Radio and Visual Services Division, External Relations Division, and the Economic and Social Information Unit.

The first priority in the work of the Press and Publications Division is to provide, both at headquarters and in the field, support to representatives of international and national information media and outlets. At United Nations Headquarters and at the United Nations Office at Geneva, this support takes the form of both physical facilities and material services. In other areas it takes the form of material services through the United Nations Information Centres.

The larger news bureaus at headquarters are provided with individual offices, whereas other correspondents share office space. For correspondents who are temporarily accredited, there is a general work area with tables and typewriters. The General Assembly Hall, council chambers, and committee rooms have special areas reserved for correspondents. Other physical facilities for correspondents include a documents service, offices for commercial cable companies, and arrangements whereby correspondents can listen in their offices to debates and discussions in the various council chambers and committee rooms.

The material services provided to correspondents in New York take the form basically of press releases and briefings. The press releases cover all principal United Nations meetings. Releases on the plenary sessions of the General Assembly, the meetings of the Security Council, and on one or more of the main committees of the Assembly are issued in the form of "takes"—which provide an unofficial running summary of the meeting concerned. Coverage of other meetings at headquarters, at Geneva, or in the field usually takes the form of a single release that is prepared as soon as possible at the end of the morning and afternoon sessions of the committee, commission, or council concerned. Additionally, press releases are issued on other major events, United Nations reports, United Nations missions overseas, activities of the specialized agencies, projects of the United Nations Development Programme, and so on. More than 3000 press releases, notes to correspondents, background releases, and feature articles are issued annually at United Nations Headquarters. A number of these, selected on the basis of regional and local interest, are reproduced at United Nations Information Centres, many of which also produce weekly or biweekly news summaries of United Nations activities.

The Secretary-General holds periodic press conferences. Additionally, as developments warrant, senior officials of the secretariat are invited to meet representatives of information media for formal press conferences or background briefings. Particular stress is given in such meetings to work in the fields of economic and social development and human rights. Senior officials of the specialized agencies visiting New York or the United Nations Office at Geneva are similarly invited to hold press conferences or briefings as their schedules permit.

To meet the operational needs of correspondents, a daily noon briefing is conducted at headquarters by two senior information officers. Current developments and meeting schedules are reviewed, statements attributable to a United Nations spokesman are issued, and the correspondents are afforded an opportunity to put questions concerning current matters.

The Office of Public Information also provides facilities for press conferences or briefings by permanent representatives, foreign ministers, heads of government, or other visiting dignitaries. Such press conferences or briefings may be requested several times a week during the General Assembly and at less frequent intervals during other periods of the year. Although the Office of Public Information provides the facilities for such conferences, OPI does not accept any responsibility for the content of a delegation press conference, nor does it issue to correspondents a release summarizing the proceedings.

Accredited to the United Nations on a permanent basis at headquarters are some 300 correspondents representing news agencies, newspapers, and radio and television services throughout the world. In addition to this permanent corps there is a more shifting group of approximately 300 to 350 correspondents who are accredited on a "temporary" basis and who report developments sporadically. During periods of more than usual news interest—such as sessions of the General Assembly or the Security Council—an additional 150 to 200 temporary correspondents may be accredited. On special occasions the total number of accreditations, permanent or temporary, has risen as high as

2000. At the United Nations Office at Geneva, there is a smaller corps of accredited correspondents. For special conferences at Geneva, such as the Conference on Peaceful Uses of Atomic Energy and Conference on Trade and Development, several hundred additional correspondents may be given temporary facilities. The information centers do not maintain a system of formal accreditation but are in regular contact with press, radio, and television correspondents in their respective areas.

In addition to the activities described above, which are geared to providing support and services for existing international and national agencies of information, the Press and Publications Division also has a positive information program, by way of a supplemental service that falls into two broad categories: (a) publications, mainly intended for sale, produced on a recurring and regularly scheduled basis—the *United Nations Yearbook* and the *United Nations Monthly Chronicle*; and (b) leaflets, booklets, pamphlets, and reprints, intended essentially for free distribution, on a varying list of subjects and titles determined on an *ad hoc* basis.

The *United Nations Yearbook,* as an encyclopedia of the organization's aims and activities, serves as the memory of the United Nations for the general public. It is an annual volume of some 800 to 1000 pages containing a condensed and documented account, for reference purposes, of the activities of the United Nations in all of its fields of involvement and concern. Separate chapters are devoted to the work of each of the specialized agencies.

At the present time the *Yearbook* is produced in English only, under a copublishing arrangement with Columbia University Press. The press run averages 6500 copies.

The *United Nations Monthly Chronicle* was instituted in 1964 to supersede the *United Nations Review*. It is designed as a monthly record of both thought and action within the United Nations, in all its fields of preoccupation—political, legal, economic, social, trusteeship, budgetary, and so on. Like the *Yearbook,* the *Chronicle* is intended to serve as a basic reference tool with emphasis, in this case, on the needs of those who require a more frequent and continuing documentary record of United Nations activities in their own work or those who desire it because of their interest in these activities—diplomats, journalists, editorial writers, professors and students of international law, members of nongovernmental organizations, and so on. The *Chronicle* also carries signed articles by heads of various substantive departments and by elected officials of the United Nations family on matters of current significance.

The *Chronicle* is produced in an English edition at headquarters, in French from Paris, and in Spanish from Mexico City. The current circulation of the three editions is 20,000, 3000, and 2500, respectively.

In addition to the *Yearbook* and the *Chronicle,* the Press and Publications Division, as indicated above, also produces each year a selected list of pamphlets, leaflets, booklets, and reprints of varying length on different subjects.

In the selection of titles OPI attempts to meet two separate but equally important needs: (a) providing for free distribution to interested groups and individuals, both at headquarters and through the information centers, material of basic informational value dealing with the structure and functions of the organization, such as "Basic Facts"; "The United Nations, What It Is and What It Does"; and "The Regional Economic Commissions"; and (b) accommodating directives and mandates from the General Assembly and other organs of the United Nations to give special emphasis in the Office of Public Information programs to selected themes and subjects such as decolonization, disarmament, racial equality, apartheid, economic and social development, and international law.

Information centers, and particularly those in developing regions, are provided with limited budgetary appropriations to reproduce selected leaflets, pamphlets, and booklets in local languages as well as to prepare special material on the United Nations of particular national or regional interest.

In addition to the publications that the Office of Public Information issues under its own imprint and from its own budgetary resources, the Press and Publications Division undertakes to stimulate the production of similar books by outside authors, publishing houses, and institutions. To this end, the Office of Public Information almost since its inception has considered it one of its important responsibilities to maintain and develop liaison with independent authors and publishers and to give them assistance in producing books on the United Nations and its related family of agencies. Such assistance has ranged from the provision of source materials and ideas to active collaboration in the planning and execution of books, with editorial and substantive guidance at all stages. When such books have been produced on the initiative of the United Nations, and under its policy and editorial guidance, they have qualified for formal United Nations endorsement. In recent years a number of such volumes have appeared under the imprint both of publishers in the United States and abroad and have contributed substantially to a wider understanding of the aims and activities of the organization.

The Radio and Visual Services Division provides support for international and national radio and visual organizations and produces material in implementation of the basic principle that the Office of Public Information should undertake, on its own initiative, positive information activities to supplement the services of existing agencies.

In the field of radio, the Radio and Visual Services Division assists national radio organizations, particularly in the developing areas, in their coverage of all aspects of the United Nations. This assistance includes the provision of facilities to correspondents in New York and in Geneva for the coverage of meetings, including studio time and facilities. Shortwave broadcasts of major meetings are scheduled so that national broadcasting organizations may monitor or relay the proceedings. The Radio and Visual Services Division also provides audio material from its archives for use in production of programs on the United Nations by national radio outlets.

Radio programs produced by the United Nations itself consist of regular news summaries of varying length, news magazines, features, and documentaries. Some 99 member states and 28 other states and territories undertake to broadcast the programs, which are provided in 27 languages.

In accordance with the resolutions of the General Assembly and of other organs, special attention is given in radio features, documentaries, and news summaries to such current subjects as decolonization, racial discrimination, apartheid, economic and social development, and human rights.

The continued growth of television as a major medium of information has resulted in increased demands from national television services throughout the world for assistance from the Office of Public Information. In recent years the advent of satellite transmissions to Europe and Asia has made it possible for audiences in these two continents to view live or delayed transmissions of important meetings or events at United Nations Headquarters. In 1965, for example, at the time of the visit of His Holiness Pope Paul VI to the United Nations, satellite transmission with 12 language versions was made available to all members of the Eurovision and Intervision networks.

United Nations television services are called on regularly to provide programs and news material to practically all existing television organizations. Additionally, studio and camera facilities are made available to accredited television correspondents.

Feature programs for showing by television stations throughout the world are produced by the United Nations in a number of language versions. The "International Zone" series, consisting of 13 half-hour programs annually and emphasizing United Nations activities in the field of economic and social development, is purchased by television outlets in some 20 countries.

For several years the Radio and Visual Services Division has undertaken to produce a series of basic informational films for group showings and for telecasting on the major organs and agencies of the United Nations family. In recent years these productions have covered the General Assembly, the Security Council, the Economic and Social Council, UNESCO, ILO, UNICEF, the United Nations Development Programme, and other United Nations-related organs.

Film crews are regularly sent to the field to obtain coverage of important United Nations conferences and development projects assisted by the organization. The footage is used in the preparation of the "International Zone" series and the basic informational films, as well as being made available to independent film and television organizations producing films on United Nations subjects.

Still-photographic coverage of United Nations activities is another major activity of the Radio and Visual Services Division. Some 5000 selected negatives are accessioned annually by the

United Nations Photo Library. These include not only regular coverage of activities in New York and at the United Nations Office at Geneva, but also photos of projects and conferences of United Nations concern throughout the world. The Photographs and Exhibits Service is also responsible for assistance to the still photographers from newspapers and agencies who come to New York to cover meetings and special events.

Prints of United Nations photographs are made available for publication purposes to newspapers, periodicals, and book publishers, as well as governmental information services, not only through the master collection at headquarters, but also through the more limited photo libraries that are maintained by the information centers. Additionally, the photographs are used in the production of wall sheets and photo display sets that are issued with captions in a number of languages for worldwide distribution.

The functions of the External Relations Division are essentially directed outwards: through the extension of the work of the Office of Public Information to all areas of the world by means of a network of United Nations Information Centres; and through services to educational institutions, nongovernmental organizations, and to the general public.

One of the earliest recommendations of the General Assembly regarding United Nations public information activities concerned the establishment of information centers "in order to ensure that peoples in all parts of the world should receive as full information as possible about the United Nations." In recent years the recommendations of the assembly have been that in the opening of new centers priority should be given to areas of the world in which media of information are less developed. At the present time there are 49 information centers serving 102 countries as well as a number of trust and nonself-governing territories.

A typical information center is a microcosm of all the main functions of the Office of Public Information itself, extending to its own locality services in the fields of press, publications, radio, television, films, graphics and exhibitions, public liaison, and reference. Backed by pertinent services from headquarters, center directors are able to establish direct contacts with representatives of the local press, broadcasting organizations, and other information media, with educational and government officials, and with nongovernmental organizations to enlist their aid in bringing about "an informed understanding of the work and purposes of the organization among the peoples of the world."

Centers maintain reference libraries of U.N. documents and publications for use by students, writers, and scholars, and also reply to public inquiries from their area regarding United Nations activities. In addition to translating and adapting U.N. pamphlets, leaflets, and booklets for local use, they encourage the production of literature about the United Nations by governments and nongovernmental organizations in the countries they serve. The centers are also active in promoting and assisting in the worldwide observance of such anniversaries as United Nations Day and Human Rights Day.

A relatively new and growing aspect of the work of information centers is the sending back of information to headquarters. In addition to the coverage of U.N. activities in their own regions for release and redissemination at headquarters, the centers report regularly on local editorial or official comment on matters of interest to the United Nations.

Information centers are established at the request of host governments after taking into account both the directives of the General Assembly concerning the location of new centers and the budgetary limitations of the Office of Public Information. An information center may serve a single country, or, more frequently, a group of contiguous countries. In recent years, in view of the limitations on personnel and financial resources, several centers in developing countries have been operated in close cooperation with the United Nations Development Programme. Under these arrangements, the UNDP resident representative assumes additional duties as director of the center and is assisted by a locally recruited information assistant, as well as the necessary secretarial and clerical staff.

The United Nations Information Centre for the United States was established in 1946. Although located in Washington, only 220 miles from United Nations Headquarters in New York, it provides a variety of services to a wide international clientele. It is only natural that Congressional quarters avail themselves of the center's facilities to follow in detail the developments of the world organization. This results in one of the absorbing activities in which the center is engaged. Additionally, there are in Washington numerous national and international organizations, as well as a vast academic community. National labor leaders, nongovernmental organizations' representatives, and students and professors of 35 universities, with their own particular interests, have the opportunity for direct access to the manifold activities of the United Nations through the information center. In this connection a sustained effort is made to supplement the documents the center releases on a regular basis with background material and information resulting from research.

In the field of teaching about the United Nations, the Office of Public Information is guided in its work by a series of resolutions by the General Assembly and the Economic and Social Council. These resolutions recognize that the primary responsibility for such teaching rests on the member states themselves and their educational institutions. The role of the Office of Public Information is necessarily a subsidiary one—of stimulating further interest and action in teaching about the United Nations among educational authorities, institutions, and organizations in member states, and of providing them with supporting facilities and services.

In carrying out these responsibilities the Educational Liaison Section of the External Relations Division has concentrated its effort in recent years in providing opportunities for persons responsible for the preparation of instructional materials in the social sciences and in international affairs to observe and study the United Nations at first hand and by assisting them in securing the necessary source materials to develop teaching materials in terms of their own curricula and needs.

With this in mind, a series of seminars for textbook writers were organized under a continuing program known as the Triangular Fellowships. In 1965 textbook writers from 12 English-speaking countries, and in 1966 textbook writers from 18 Spanish-speaking countries, were brought to United Nations Headquarters for a series of lectures, discussions, and workshop sessions. During 1967 a similar program was conducted at the United

Nations Office at Geneva and at UNESCO Headquarters in Paris for textbook writers from French-speaking areas.

These seminars for textbook writers, which are conducted in close collaboration with UNESCO, have already resulted in several manuscripts that, when published as textbooks, will considerably alleviate what has been described in reports to the Economic and Social Council as a serious shortage of instructional material on the aims, activities, and accomplishments of the United Nations and its related agencies.

In the field of higher education, two parallel intern programs for college and university students are conducted during the summer months by the External Relations Division. One is held at United Nations Headquarters and the other at the United Nations Office in Geneva. Both programs are designed to provide an opportunity for outstanding students from various countries, specializing in such fields as international relations, law, economics, and related subjects, to study the United Nations and its related agencies at first hand through briefiings, group discussions, attendance at meetings, and individual study projects. Participants are nominated by member governments or by the colleges and universities they are attending, and the programs are conducted without direct cost to the United Nations.

The important role of nongovernmental organizations in promoting an informed understanding of the work and purposes of the organization has also been stressed in numerous resolutions of the General Assembly. The Office of Public Information has, for its part, been requested to "enlist the cooperation" of nongovernmental organizations and to "assist and encourage them" in spreading information about the United Nations.

The assistance regularly provided by the Office of Public Information to nongovernmental organizations includes the provision of public information material produced for global consumption; weekly briefings at headquarters and periodically at the United Nations Office in Geneva; an annual conference of nongovernmental organizations at headquarters; regular contacts with nongovernmental organizations in the field by information center directors. The nongovernmental organizations have responded by helping to distribute Office of Public

Information material (in some cases reproducing this material at their own expense); by carrying articles on the United Nations in their house organs and magazines; by conducting programs and study groups on United Nations subjects; by organizing observances for United Nations and Human Rights Day; and by promoting activities in support of such special campaigns as World Refugee Year, Freedom from Hunger, and International Cooperation Year.

In New York some 200 nongovernmental organizations are listed with the Office of Public Information. Their representatives have the use of the Non-Governmental Organizations Lounge, which is stocked with United Nations press releases, documents, and periodicals, as well as pamphlets produced by some of the specialized agencies. An average of 100 representatives attend the weekly briefings on current topics by senior secretariat or agency staff. The services of the Non-Governmental Organizations Section, which is part of the External Relations Division, includes working with individual nongovernmental organizations on programs that involve the aims, structure, and activities of the United Nations or the specialized agencies.

Since the very beginning of the organization, the Office of Public Information has had to meet many hundreds of thousands of inquiries from people in all parts of the world covering a wide range of subjects. It also serves an increasing number of visitors who wish to see the United Nations at first hand.

The Public Services Section of the External Relations Division handles relations with the public at headquarters. The guided tours of the headquarters buildings that were inaugurated in 1952 now handle more than 1 million visitors annually. Visitors are given a one-hour tour of the main public areas, Assembly Hall, council chambers, and so on, by specially trained guides. The visitors, who come from many countries, represent a broad cross section of society, ranging from cabinet ministers to elementary school children. A considerable proportion of tour visitors to headquarters come in organized groups by advance reservation.

A separate activity, but one closely connected to the guided tours, is the arrangement for visiting groups involving special briefings and the provision of United Nations speakers. More than 110,000 persons participate in such programs at headquarters annually. Additionally, secretariat speakers regularly are requested to fill speaking engagements before various groups.

Reference has been made above to the inquiries received from the public concerning all aspects of United Nations activities. At headquarters these are handled by the Public Inquiries Unit, which services nearly 100,000 inquiries annually, mostly by mail. The information centers handle a considerable volume of public inquiries from their respective areas, and, both at the United Nations Office at Geneva and the headquarters of the Regional Economic Commissions, provisions are made for special programs for visiting groups.

With the growth of the technical assistance and special fund programs (now amalgamated into the United Nations Development Programme), and with the proclamation by the General Assembly of the United Nations Development Decade, the Office of Public Information undertook to intensify and expand the preparation and dissemination of information on the economic and social activities of the United Nations.

Among the considerations that led the Office of Public Information to reach this decision was a recognition of the fact that, although there is frequently a spontaneous demand from information media for United Nations political news, this is less often the case with news relating to economic and social development. United Nations political news, generally speaking, finds immediate outlets, but news of United Nations activities in the economic and social fields requires greater and more purposeful preparation as well as a more selective and well-directed distribution.

Accordingly, in 1962 an Economic and Social Information Unit was established in the Office of the Under-Secretary for Public Information. On a day-to-day basis the unit maintains contact with the Department of Economic and Social Affairs, the United Nations Development Programme, the Secretariat of the United Nations Conference on Trade and Development, the United Nations Industrial Development Organization, and so on, to gather information concerning current and forthcoming activities and reports. It prepares press releases, feature stories, and background notes, in cooperation with the Press and Publications Division, for distribution at headquarters and through information centers as appropriate. The unit maintains mailing lists of specialized newspapers, journals, and periodicals to which selected documentation and press releases are sent. It arranges briefings and interviews to facilitate contacts between correspondents reporting on economic and social matters and substantive officials in these fields.

Additionally the unit is responsible for the preparation of the section in the *United Nations Monthly Chronicle* devoted to economic and social subjects and also prepares leaflets and pamphlets in these fields. Further, the unit provides personnel, as required, for the coverage of international conferences such as those held on the Application of Science and Technology to Development (1963), Trade and Development (1964), the Peaceful Uses of Atomic Energy (1965), and Land Reform (1966).

Liaison officers of the Economic and Social Information Unit are assigned to the Information Service at Geneva. The unit also receives from the information centers coverage of projects in the field relating to economic and social development.

Bibliography

PRESS

Buzek, Anthony. *How the Communist Press Works.* New York: Praeger, 1964. 287 pp.

Carty, James W., Jr. *Working with the Latin American Press.* New York: Algonquin, 1966. 39 pp.

Cater, Douglass. *The Fourth Branch of Government.* Boston: Houghton Mifflin, 1959. 203 pp.

Cohen, Bernard C. *The Press and Foreign Policy.* Princeton, N.J.: Princeton University Press, 1963. 288 pp.

Desmond, Robert W. *The Press and World Affairs.* New York: Appleton-Century-Crofts, 1937. 421 pp.

Dizard, Wilson P. *Television: A World View.* Syracuse, N.Y.: Syracuse University Press, 1966. 349 pp.

Hero, A. O. *Mass Media and World Affairs.* Boston: World Peace Foundation, 1959. 187 pp.

Hiebert, Ray E., ed. *The Press in Washington.* New York: Dodd, Mead, 1966. 233 pp.

Kruglak, Theodore E. *The Two Faces of Tass.* Minneapolis: University of Minnesota Press, 1962. 263 pp.

Markham, James W. *Voices of the Red Giants.* Ames, Iowa: The Iowa State University Press, 1967. 513 pp.

Merrill, John C., Carter R. Bryan, and Marvin Alisky. *The Foreign Press.* Baton Rouge: Louisiana State University Press, 1964. 256 pp.

Pers, Anders Yngve. *The Swedish Press.* Stockholm: The Swedish Institute, 1966. 46 pp.

Reston, James. *The Artillery of the Press.* New York: Harper & Row, 1967. 116 pp.

Rivers, William L. *The Opinionmakers.* Boston: Beacon, 1965. 207 pp.

197

PUBLIC OPINION AND PROPAGANDA

Barghoorn, Frederick C. *The Soviet Cultural Offensive: The Role of Cultural Development in Soviet Foreign Policy.* Princeton, N.J.: Princeton University Press, 1960. 329 pp.

――――. *Soviet Foreign Propaganda.* Princeton, N.J.: Princeton University Press, 1964. 329 pp.

――――. *The Soviet Image of the United States.* New York: Harcourt, Brace, 1950. 297 pp.

Barrett, Edward W. *Truth Is Our Weapon.* New York: Funk & Wagnalls, 1953. 355 pp.

Buchanan, William, and Hadley Cantril. *How Nations See Each Other.* Urbana: University of Illinois Press, 1953. 220 pp.

Carroll, Wallace. *Persuade or Perish.* Boston: Houghton Mifflin, 1948. 392 pp.

Childs, H. L. *Introduction to Public Opinion.* New York: Wiley, 1940. 151 pp.

Choukas, Michael. *Propaganda Comes of Age.* Washington, D.C.: Public Affairs Press, 1965. 299 pp.

Christenson, Reo M., and Robert O. McWilliams, eds. *Voice of the People.* New York: McGraw-Hill, 1962. 585 pp.

Doob, L. *Public Opinion and Propaganda.* New York: Holt, 1948. 600 pp.

Ellul, Jacques. *Propaganda: The Formation of Men's Attitudes.* New York: Knopf, 1965. 320 pp.

Greene, Felix. *A Curtain of Ignorance: How the American Public Has Been Misinformed about China.* New York: Doubleday, 1964. 340 pp.

Hennessy, Bernard C. *Public Opinion.* Belmont, Calif.: Wadsworth, 1965. 376 pp.

Inkeles, Alex. *Public Opinion in Soviet Russia: A Study in Mass Persuasion.* Cambridge, Mass.: Harvard University Press, 1951. 397 pp.

Jefkins, Frank. *Public Relations in World Marketing.* London: Crosby Lockwood, 1966. 212 pp.

Lane, Robert E., and David O. Sears. *Public Opinion.* Englewood Cliffs, N.J.: Prentice-Hall, 1965. 120 pp.

Lippmann, Walter. *Public Opinion.* New York: Harcourt, Brace, 1922. 427 pp.

MacDougall, Curtis D. *Understanding Public Opinion.* Dubuque, Iowa: Brown, 1966. 582 pp.

Martin, L. John. *International Propaganda, Its Legal and Diplomatic Control.* Minneapolis: University of Minnesota Press, 1958. 284 pp.

Meyerhoff, Arthur E. *The Strategy of Persuasion.* New York: Coward-McCann, 1965. 191 pp.

Ogilvy-Webb, Marjorie. *The Government Explains: A Study of the Information Services.* London: Allen & Unwin, 1965. 229 pp.

Oliver, Robert T. *Culture and Communication.* Springfield, Ill.: Thomas, 1962. 165 pp.

Rutgers University. Department of Sociology. *The Image of the Voice of America as Drawn in Soviet Media.* New Brunswick, N.J.: Prepared for Office of Research and Intelligence, U. S. Information Agency, June, 1954. 34 pp. (Multilith.)

Smith, Bruce L., and Chitra M. Smith. *International Communication and Political Opinion*. Princeton, N.J.: Princeton University Press, 1956. (Microfilm.)

Thomson, Charles A. H. *Overseas Information Service of the United States Government*. Washington, D.C.: The Brookings Institution, 1948. 397 pp.

Urban, George R., ed. *Scaling the Wall: Talking to Eastern Europe*. Detroit: Wayne State University Press, 1964. 303 pp.

Whitaker, Urban G., Jr., ed. *Propaganda and International Relations*. San Francisco: Chandler, 1960. 160 pp.

Whitton, John Boardman, ed. *Propaganda and the Cold War*. Washington, D.C.: Public Affairs Press, 1963. 119 pp.

Yu, Frederick T. C. *Mass Persuasion in Communist China*. New York: Praeger, 1964. 196 pp.

Zeman, Z. A. B. *Nazi Propaganda*. New York: Oxford University Press, 1964. 226 pp.

DIPLOMACY

Black, Eugene R. *The Diplomacy of Economic Development*. Cambridge, Mass.: Harvard University Press, 1960. 74 pp.

Coyle, David C. *United Nations and How it Works*. New York: Columbia University Press, 1965. 256 pp.

Dallin, David J. *Soviet Foreign Policy After Stalin*. Philadelphia: Lippincott, 1960. 543 pp.

Graebner, Norman A. *Cold War Diplomacy: American Foreign Policy, 1945-1960*. Princeton, N.J.: Van Nostrand, 1962. 192 pp.

Guerrant, Edward O. *Modern American Diplomacy*. Albuquerque: University of New Mexico Press, 1954. 318 pp.

Kaznacheev, Aleksandr. *Inside a Soviet Embassy*. Philadelphia: Lippincott, 1962. 250 pp.

Kennan, George F. *American Diplomacy: 1900-1950*. Chicago: University of Chicago Press, 1951. 154 pp.

Lerche, Charles O., and Abdul A. Said. *Concepts of International Politics*. Englewood Cliffs, N.J.: Prentice-Hall, 1963. 314 pp.

Morgenthau, Hans J. *Politics Among Nations*. New York: Knopf, 1960. 630 pp.

Nicolson, Sir Harold G. *Diplomacy*. New York: Oxford University Press, 1963. 268 pp.

Plischke, Elmer. *Conduct of American Diplomacy*. Princeton, N.J.: Van Nostrand, 1967. 677 pp.

Satow, Ernest M. *Guide to Diplomatic Practice*. London: Longmans Green, 1957. 510 pp.

Thayer, Charles W. *Diplomat*. New York: Harper & Brothers, 1959. 299 pp.

Webster, Sir Charles. *The Art and Practice of Diplomacy*. New York: Barnes & Noble, 1962. 246 pp.

Williams, William Appleman, ed. *The Shaping of American Diplomacy*. Chicago: Rand McNally, 1956. 1130 pp.

Index